GLYPH

NAOKO FUJIMOTO

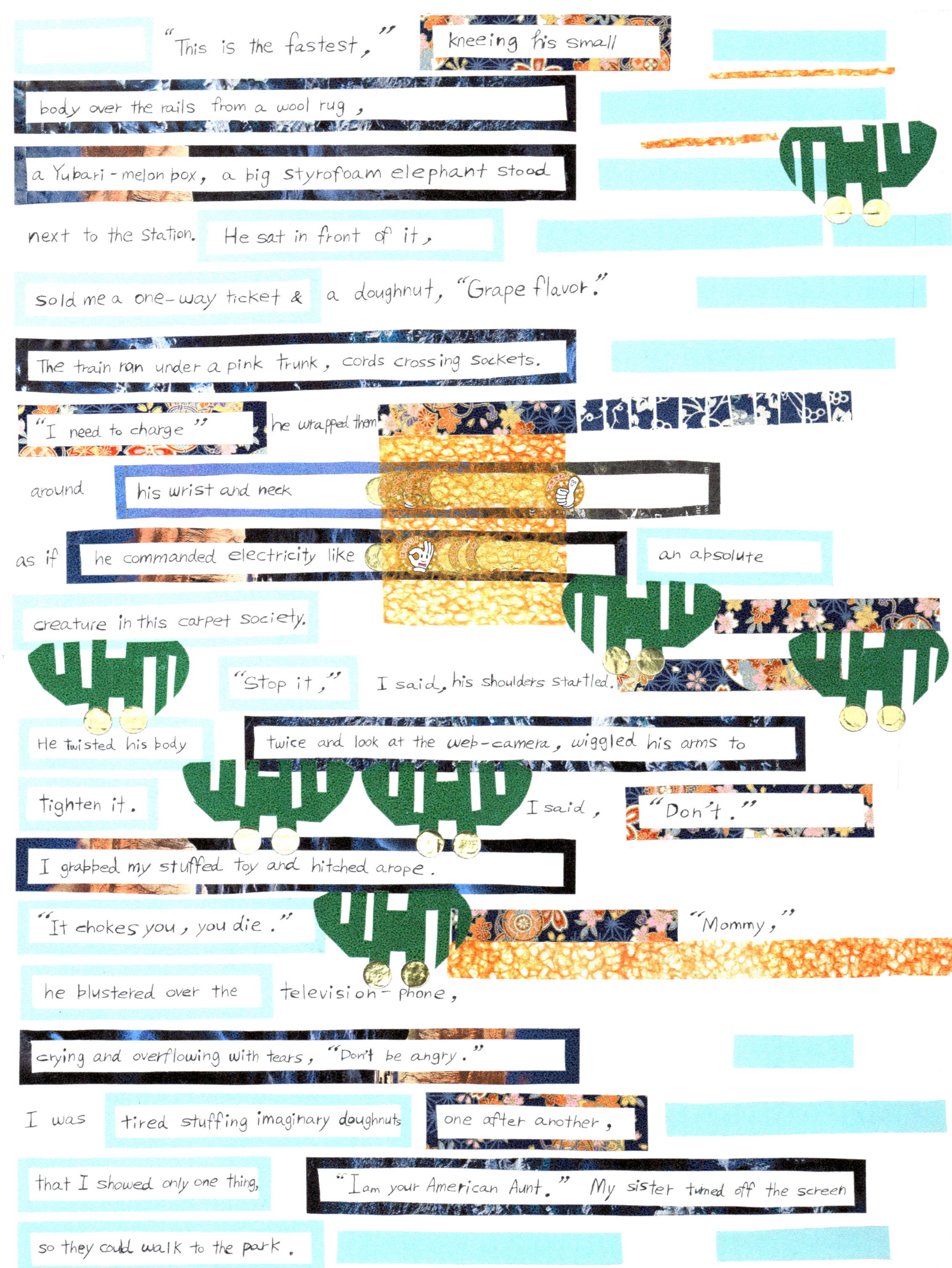

Naoko Fujimoto Oct 2017

GLYPH

NAOKO FUJIMOTO

GRAPHIC POETRY = TRANS. SENSORY

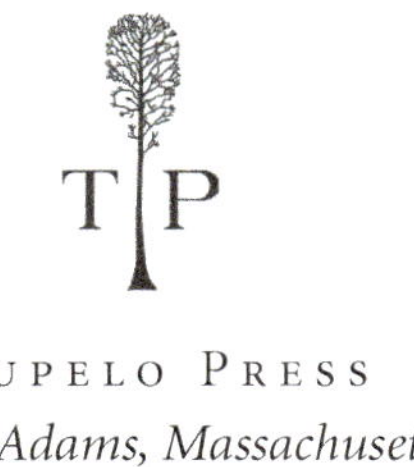

TUPELO PRESS

North Adams, Massachusetts

Library of Congress Control Number: 2021930386
isbn: 978-1-946482-52-5

Cover and text design by Dede Cummings

First paperback edition June 2021

Tupelo Press
P.O. Box 1767, North Adams, Massachusetts 01247
(413) 664–9611 / editor@tupelopress.org / www.tupelopress.org

Tupelo Press is an award-winning independent literary press that publishes fine fiction, nonfiction, and poetry in books that are a joy to hold as well as read. Tupelo Press is a registered 501(c)(3) nonprofit organization, and we rely on public support to carry out our mission of publishing extraordinary work that may be outside the realm of the large commercial publishers. Financial donations are welcome and are tax deductible.

All artwork: Pencil, Pen, Acryl, Washi-Paper, Magazine Cutout.
Frontispiece: "Grape Flavor."

This project is supported in part by an award from the National Endowment for the Arts.

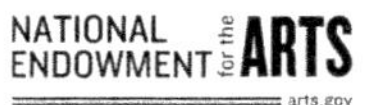

CONTENTS

vii *Introduction*

1 Radio Tower

2 Protest Against

3 Requiem From an Office 7,000 Miles Away

4 On a Black Hill

5 Foreign Grey

6 Grandfather's Left Eye

7 Infestation of River People

8 Home, No Home

9 Inconvenient History

10 From An Apartment

11 A Big Bowl of Beef Stew

12 Draw the Light

13 Unlasted Improvisation

14 Koi-Kokoro is One Step Before

15 July 2017, Skipping Stone

16 Lunch Time Atlas

17 Kapok Tree

18 Doesn't Destroy

19 Necessary Development

20 Our Fourteenth Summer

21 Natane Rain Is

22 Mugwort's Leaves

23 Japanese Apricot Wine

24 The Pay Phone

25 There Are Plenty

26 Dinner At

27 Greenhouse

28 I Eat Pig Ears in Cebu

29 The Sallie

30 I Burn the Upright Piano

31 Impossibly Long

32 Pochi or Kuro

33 White Avenue

34 A Street By Your Back Yard

35 I See

36 How to Choke Myself
      in the Ugly Kitchen

37 Kotobuki Seven

38 Phobos and Deimos

39 Dividing

40 Enough is Never

41 Childhood Advance

42 Lake Michigan

43 Happy 50th Birthday

44 More than Fourteen Days

45 August Marble

47 Afterword

49 Acknowledgments

INTRODUCTION

In 2016, I left my full-time job in the Japanese machine-tool industry. Coincidently, on the same day, Kirsten Miles was looking for additional participants for the Tupelo Press residency program at the Massachusetts Museum of Contemporary Art. Exactly one week later, I stood in front of Anselm Kiefer's large concrete pieces at the museum after having a cup of coffee with Jeffrey Levine while Cassandra Cleghorn's energetic violin played in the background.

During the residency, I spent a lot of time with Kiefer's art. The following Christmas I jokingly wished that I could get a concrete mixing set. I started searching for my "concrete," literally, for a project to start, and figuratively, for my writing project's foundation.

I grew up near the Tokugawa Art Museum, which houses a collection of the original *Tale of Genji* picture scrolls. From a very young age, I visited them with my grandmother during every limited exhibition period. Years later, I became curious about what would happen if I translated my own poems (written in English on flat paper) into words and images to create a contemporary picture scroll. At the 2016 Tupelo Press MASS MoCA residency, I made my first graphic poem.

I wanted my graphic poems to transport the viewer's senses from paper, bridging the gap between words and images with their physical counterparts. Like historical Emaki (picture scroll), my graphic poems contain side stories hidden behind the main narrative—be they comedic or serious—for the viewer to discover and interpret. Each detail (word choice, origami paper, art style, etc.) has a specific meaning to contribute to the whole.

I named the project, Graphic Poetry Is Trans. Sensory. "Trans." represents two meanings—"to translate" and "to transport." I began posting these pieces on social media for the next two years.

Four years have passed since the beginning of this project. During that time, many editors, poets, professors, students, and audiences have encouraged my work. I cannot thank them enough nor express with words how grateful I truly am.

I am especially grateful to the Tupelo team, including photographer Jim Gipe, book designer Dede Cummings, and managing editor David Rossitter, who held my hand throughout this journey. Jeffrey Levine, had I not met you in the summer of 2016, this project would never have existed. My endless thanks to you all.

NAOKO FUJIMOTO

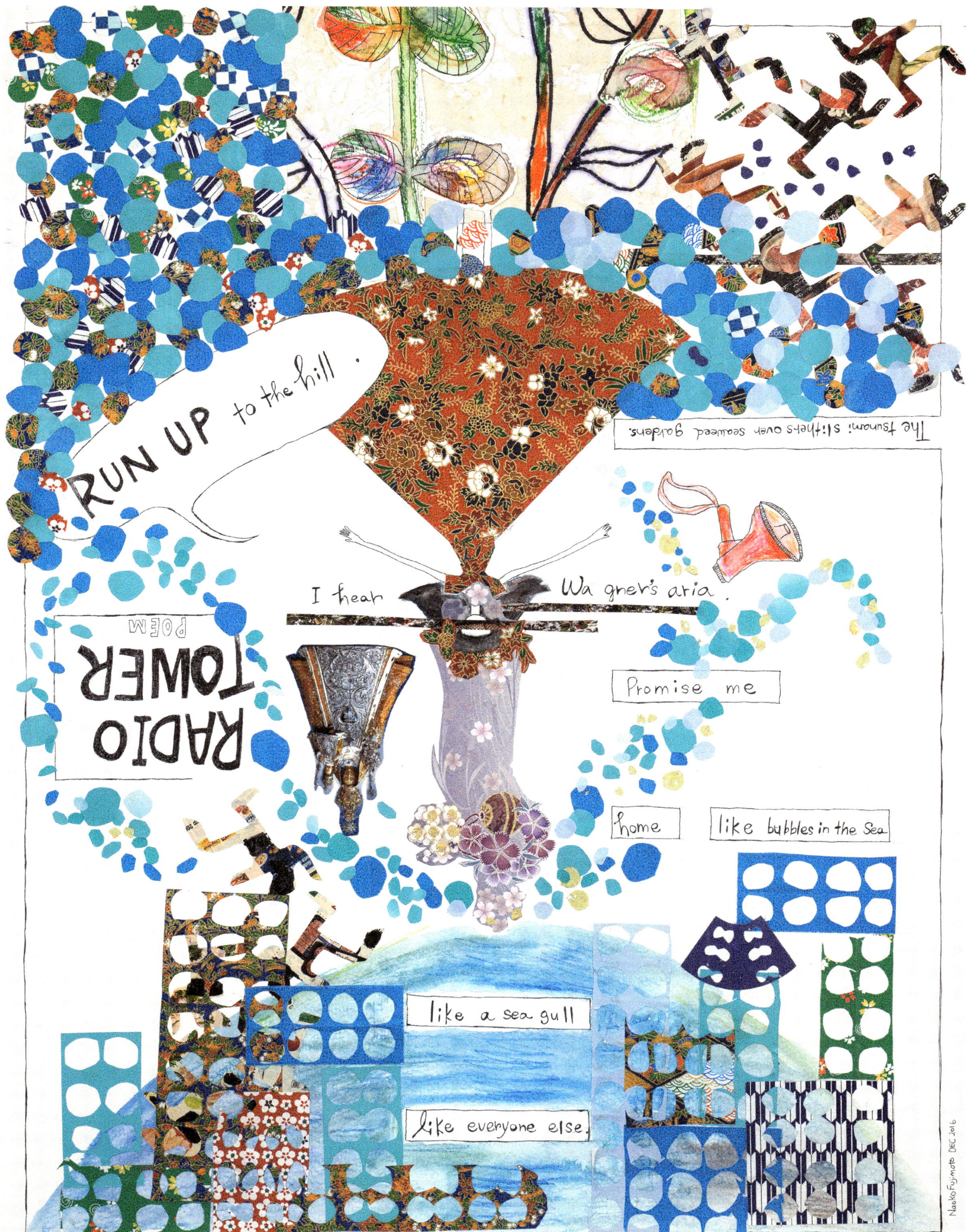
RUN UP to the hill .
The tsunami slithers over seaweed gardens.
RADIO TOWER POEM
I hear
Wagner's aria .
Promise me
home
like bubbles in the Sea
like a sea gull
like everyone else .
Naoko Fujimoto DEC 2016

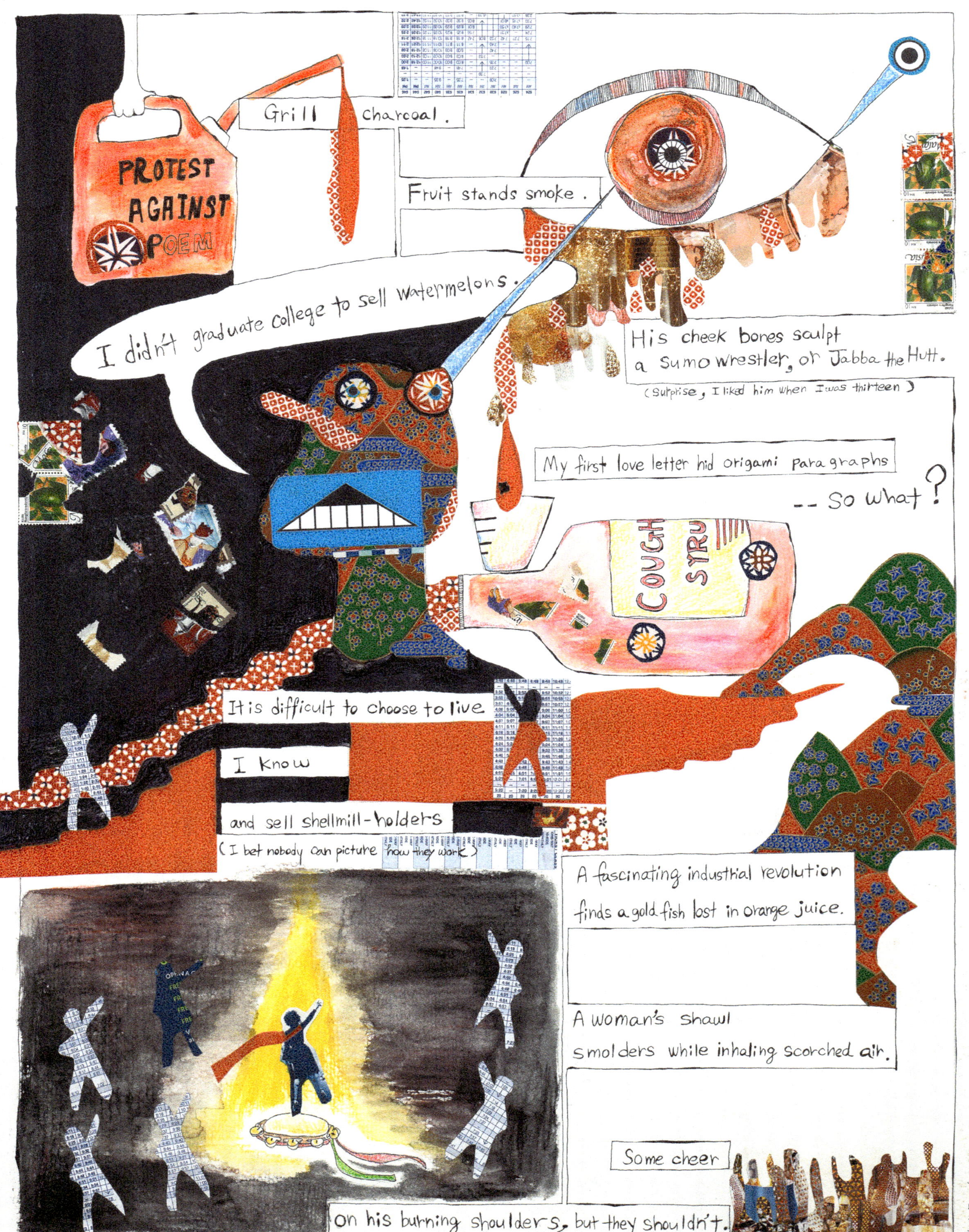

PROTEST AGAINST POEM
Grill charcoal.
Fruit stands smoke.
I didn't graduate college to sell watermelons.
His cheek bones sculpt a sumo wrestler, or Jabba the Hutt.
(Surprise, I liked him when I was thirteen)
My first love letter hid origami paragraphs
-- So what?
COUGH SYRU
It is difficult to choose to live
I know
and sell shellmill-holders
(I bet nobody can picture how they work)
A fascinating industrial revolution finds a gold fish lost in orange juice.
A woman's shawl smolders while inhaling scorched air.
Some cheer
on his burning shoulders, but they shouldn't.
Naoko Fujimoto DEC 2016

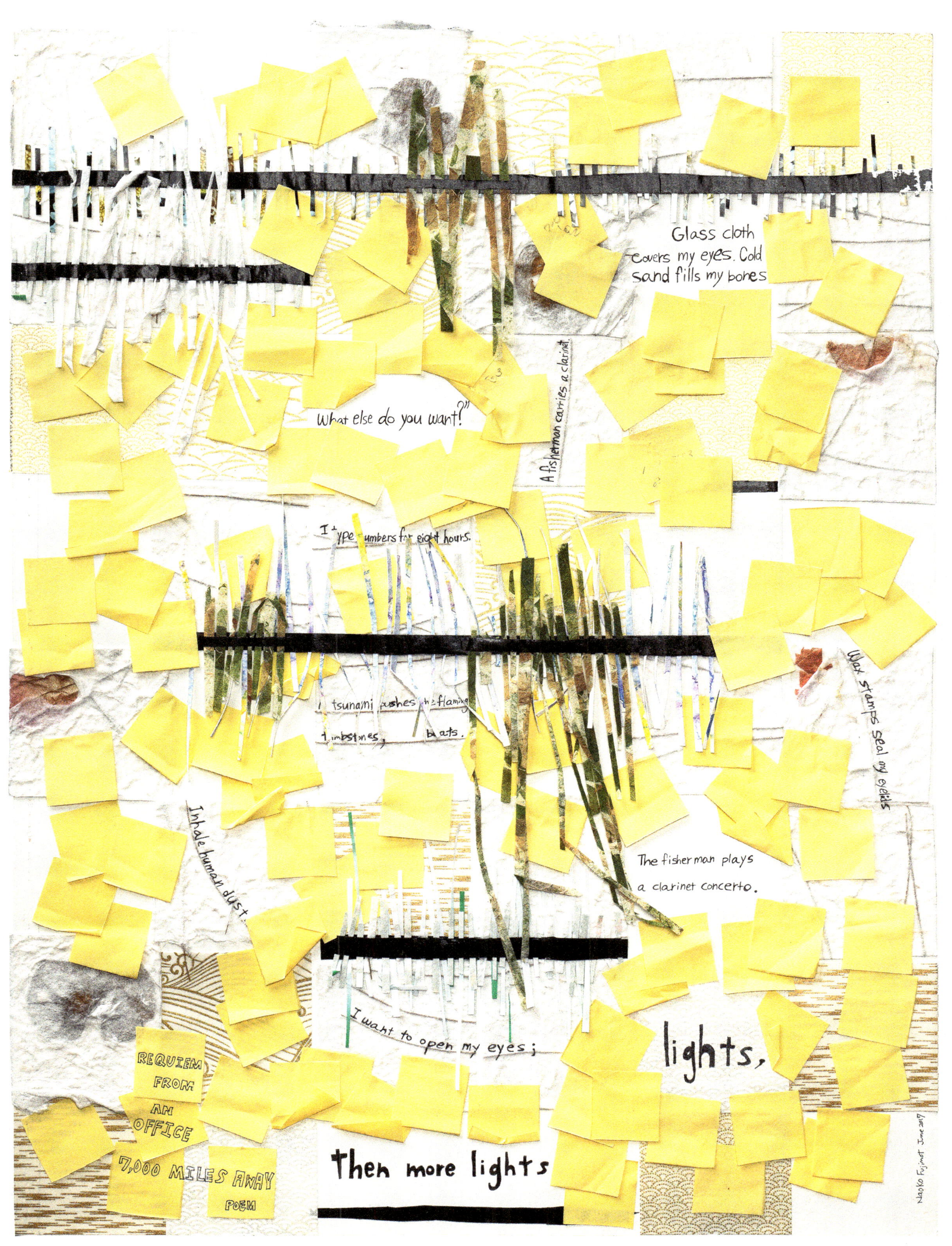

Glass cloth covers my eyes. Cold sand fills my bones
A fisherman carries a clarinet.
What else do you want?"
I type numbers for eight hours.
A tsunami pushes the flaming tombstones, boats.
Wax stamps seal my eyelids
Inhale human dust.
The fisherman plays a clarinet concerto.
I want to open my eyes;
lights,
then more lights
REQUIEM FROM AN OFFICE 7,000 MILES AWAY
POEM
Naoko Fujimot June 2017

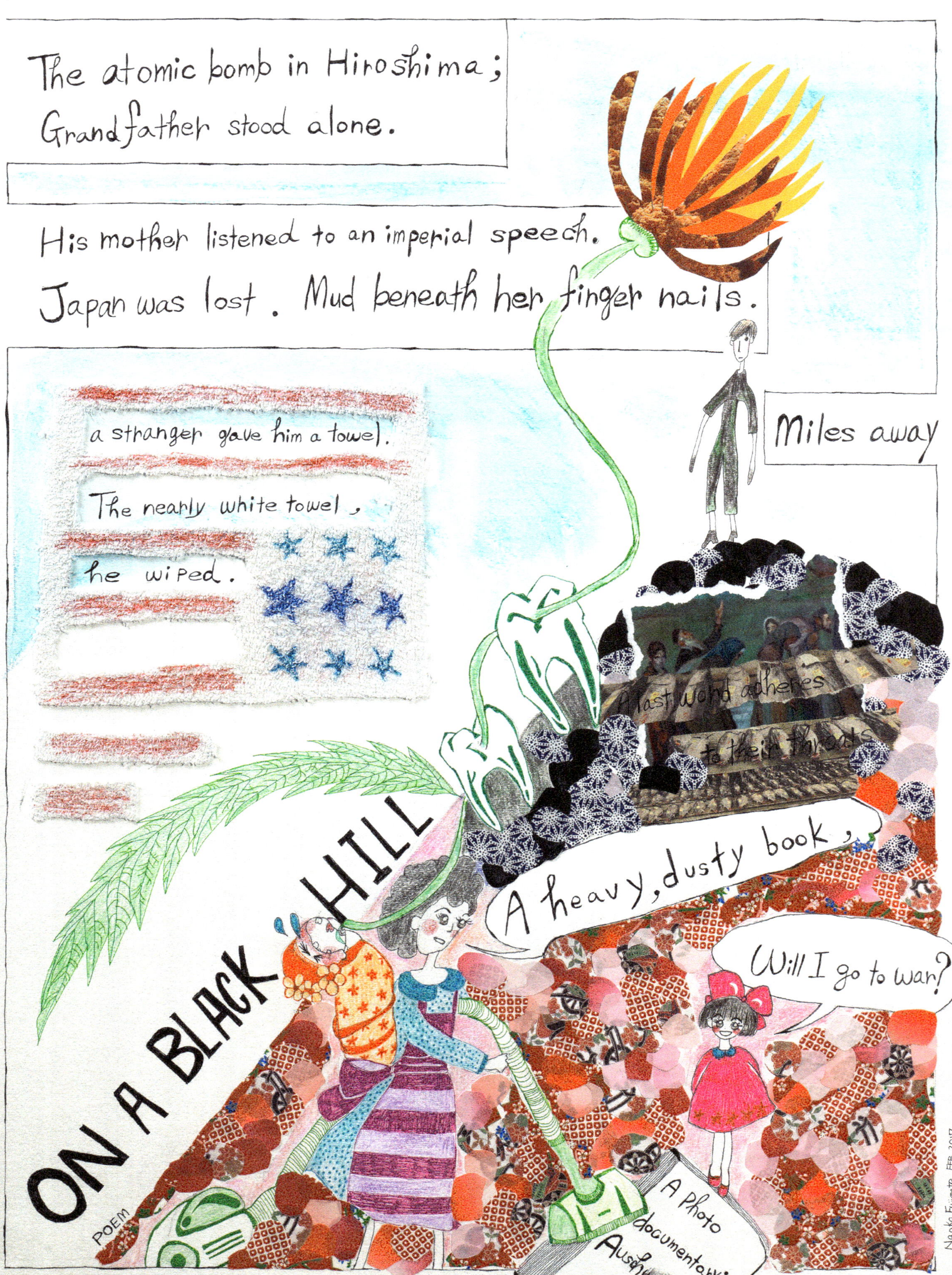
The atomic bomb in Hiroshima;
Grandfather stood alone.
His mother listened to an imperial speech.
Japan was lost. Mud beneath her finger nails.
Miles away
a stranger gave him a towel.
The nearly white towel,
he wiped.
A last word adheres
to their throats
A heavy, dusty book,
Will I go to war?
ON A BLACK HILL
POEM
A Photo documentary. Auschwitz
Naoko Fujimoto FEB 2017

~~Because~~ I'm from Fukushima, I say, I'm not / radioactive, and eat / seaweed salad from a bowl. You / hold my hands as we share these long / silences. ~~Because~~ / I'm a Buddhist, I recite, Namu-amida-butsu, at noon / over lunch, and very late at night. But I don't pray for the Japanese. I pray / for myself, ~~because~~ I crave a word / I want / it to avalanche into / my eyes / like a kaleidoscope for the dead, but the sky / glares as usual ~~because~~ I'm so / often lost in this foreign / grey. I take my two fingers and push them / into my / breasts. I say, If I / die with cancer, for example? You rub / my left breast. My / brown / nipples are so cold at 2:30A.M.

FOREIGN //

// GREY

Naoko Fujimoto MAY 2017

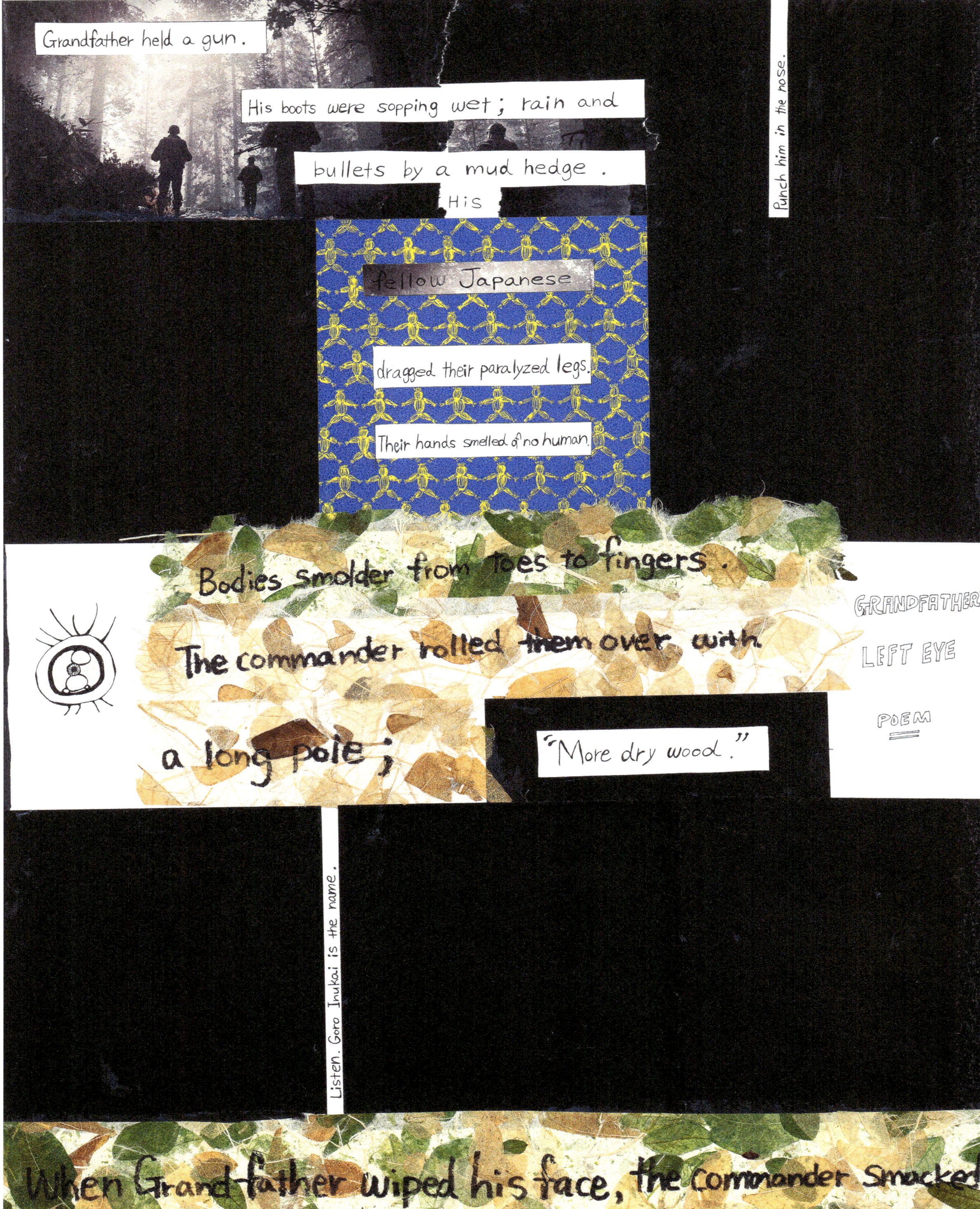

Grandfather held a gun.

His boots were sopping wet; rain and

bullets by a mud hedge. His

fellow Japanese

dragged their paralyzed legs.

Their hands smelled of no human.

Punch him in the nose.

Bodies smolder from toes to fingers.

The commander rolled them over with

a long pole;

"More dry wood."

GRANDFATHER'S
LEFT EYE
POEM

Listen. Goro Inukai is the name.

When Grandfather wiped his face, the commander smacked.

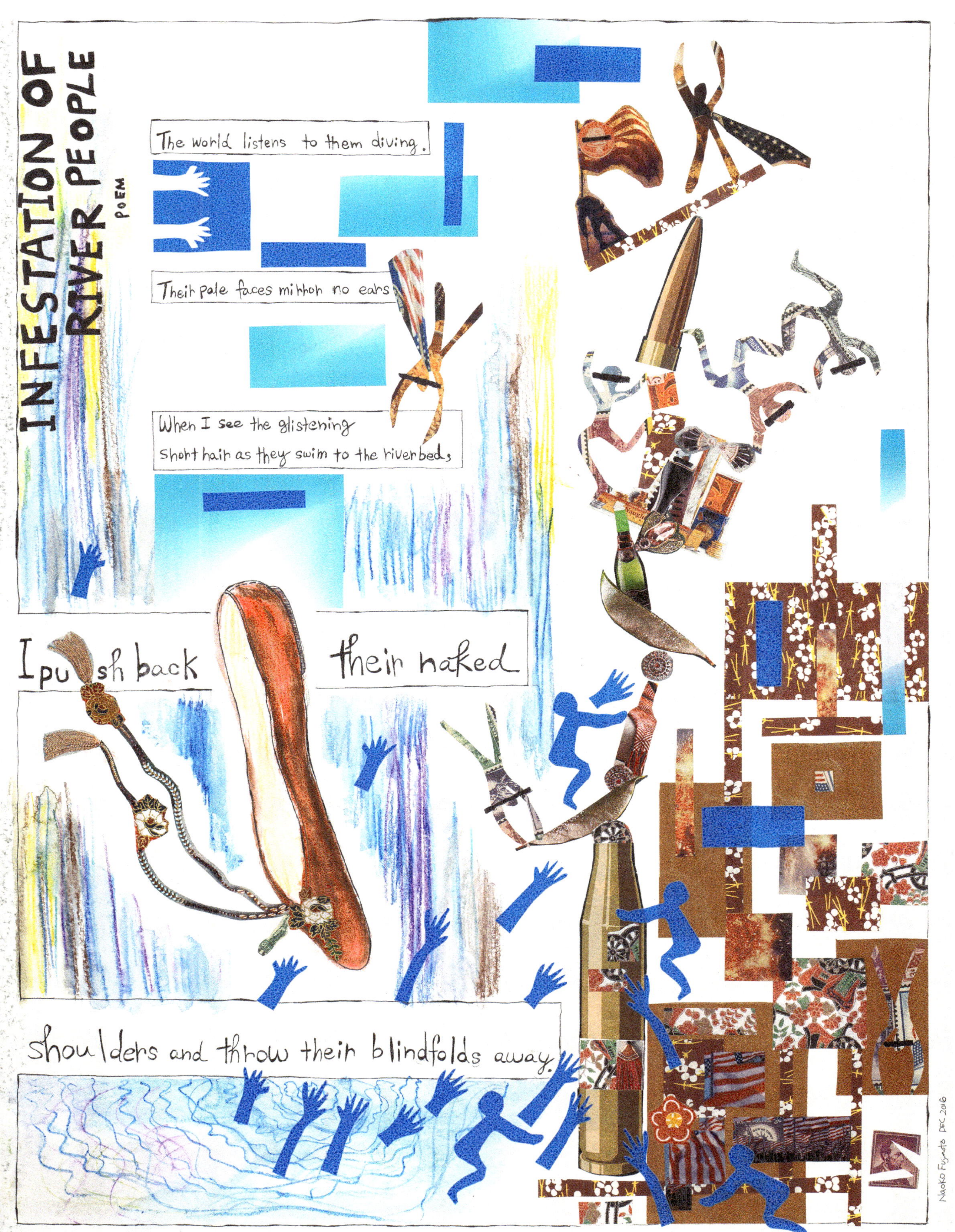

INFESTATION OF RIVER PEOPLE
POEM
The world listens to them diving.
Their pale faces mirror no ears
When I see the glistening
short hair as they swim to the riverbeds
I push back their naked
shoulders and throw their blindfolds away.
Naoko Fujimoto DEC 2016

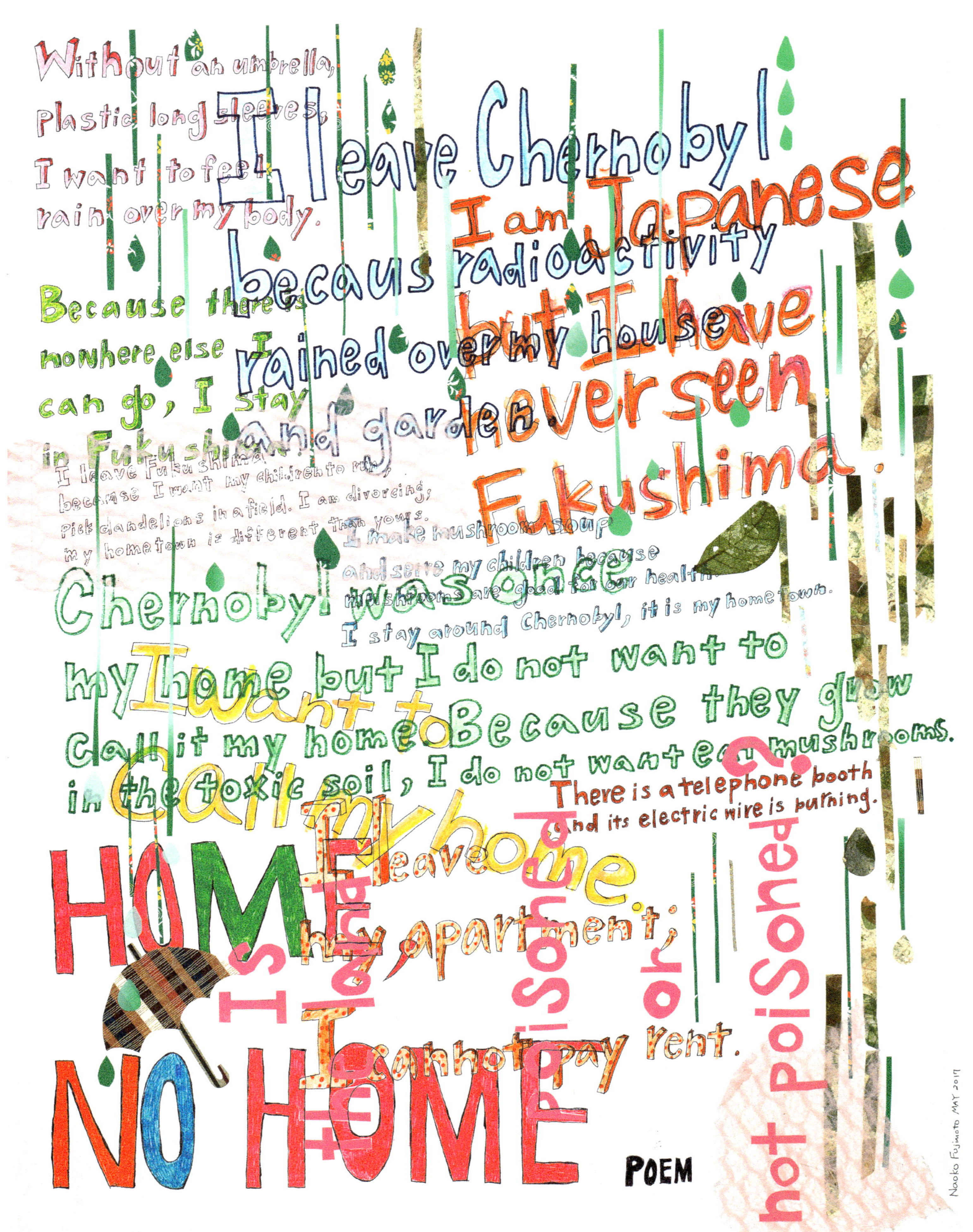
Without an umbrella,
Plastic long sleeves,
I want to feel
rain over my body.

Because there is
nowhere else I
can go, I stay

in Fukushima and garden

I leave Chernobyl
becaus radioactivity
rained over my house

I am Japanese
but I have never seen
Fukushima.

I leave Fukushima
because I want my children to run,
pick dandelions in a field. I am divorcing,
my hometown is different than yours.
I make mushroom soup
and serve my children because
mushrooms are good for our health.
I stay around Chernobyl, it is my hometown.

Chernobyl was once

my I home but I do not want to
call it my home to Because they grow
in the toxic soil, I do not want eat mushrooms.

I want

There is a telephone booth
and its electric wire is burning.

HOME is long home
I leave home
my apartment,
I cannot pay rent.
or poiSoned?

NO HOME

hot PoiSoned

POEM

Naoko Fujimoto MAY 2019

Nothing would awaken, each hair stood out
from skin, perforating the display.
The light dimmed & spotted,
unnaturally showcasing 4,000 years,
and approached us like a snake.
It chokes us without a sign,
or smell —
as if a radioactive current
swallowed,
hurting slowly inside,
to ripen our bodies.
We would not, even
when we gave up:
only the dirt takes
in these small particles.

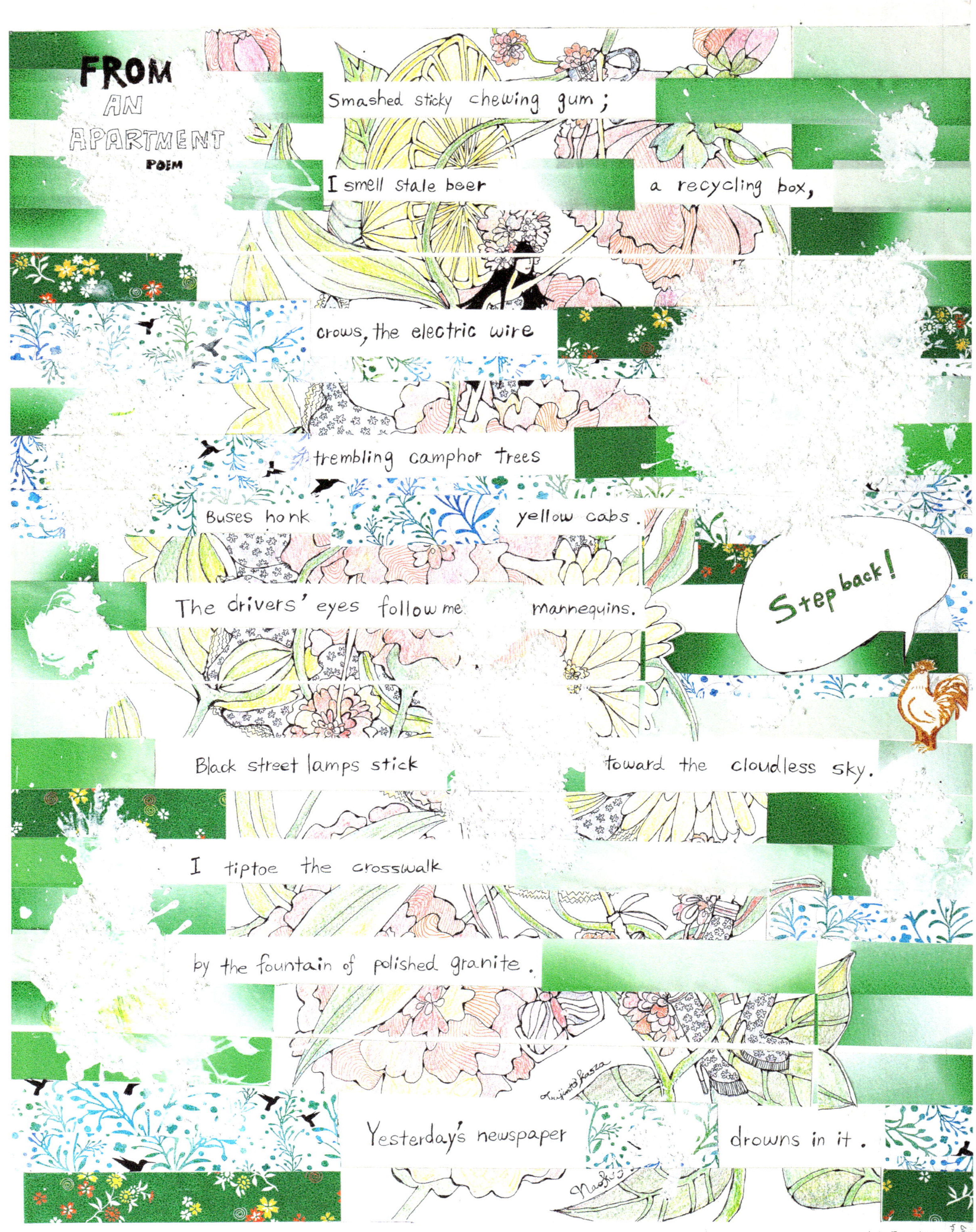

FROM
AN
APARTMENT
POEM

Smashed sticky chewing gum;

I smell stale beer   a recycling box,

crows, the electric wire

trembling camphor trees

Buses honk   yellow cabs.

The drivers' eyes follow me   mannequins.

Step back!

Black street lamps stick   toward the cloudless sky.

I tiptoe the crosswalk

by the fountain of polished granite.

Yesterday's newspaper   drowns in it.

Naoko Fujimoto

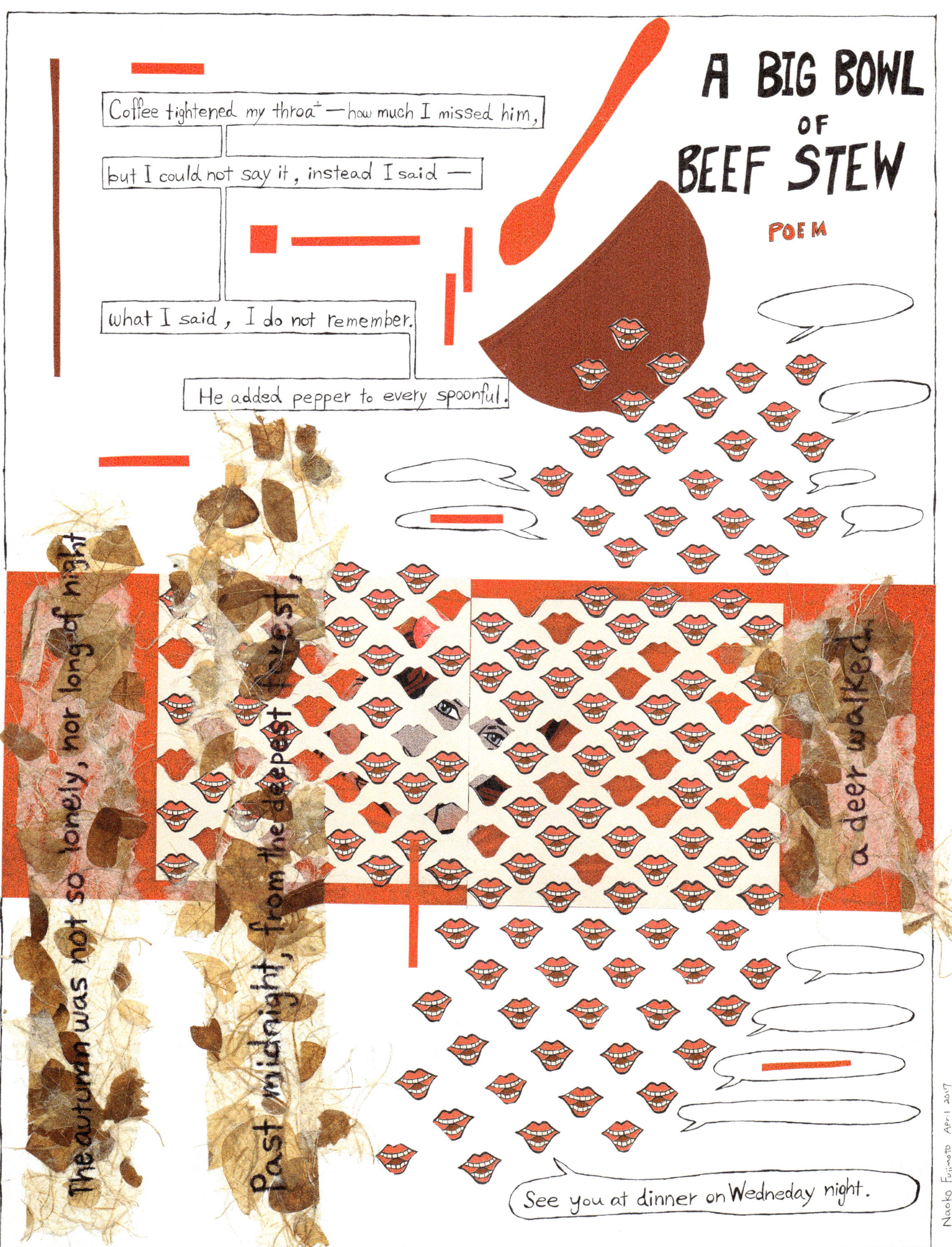

A BIG BOWL
OF
BEEF STEW
POEM

Coffee tightened my throat — how much I missed him,

but I could not say it, instead I said —

What I said, I do not remember.

He added pepper to every spoonful.

The autumn was not so lonely, nor long of night,

Past midnight, from the deepest forest,

a deer walked.

See you at dinner on Wedneday night.

Naoko Fujimoto April 2017

His breath is quiet waiting to

catch the last lightning bug.

"That is enough color to
draw the light," he
said without looking.

POEM

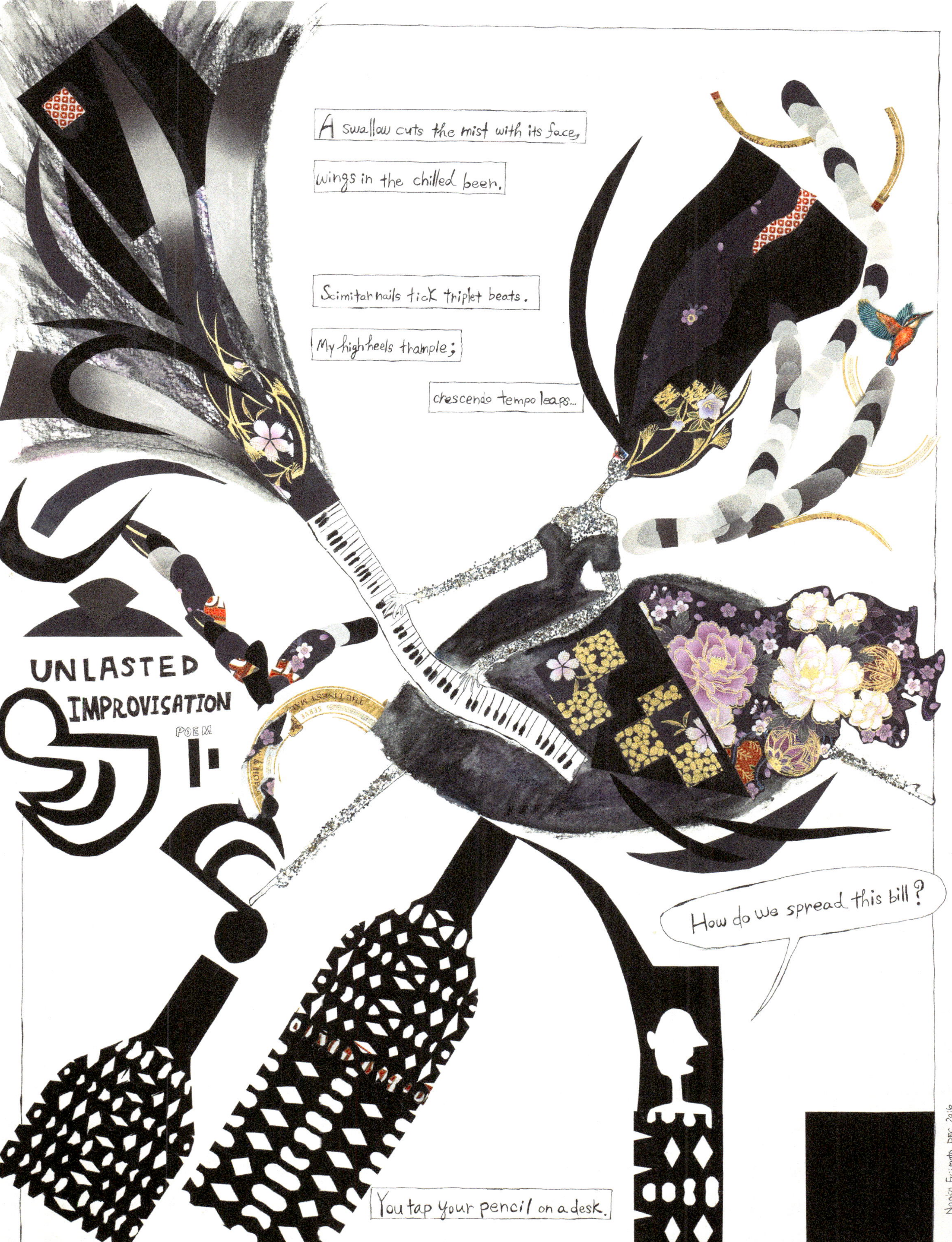

A swallow cuts the mist with its face,
wings in the chilled been.

Scimitar nails tick triplet beats.
My high heels trample;

crescendo tempo leaps...

UNLASTED
IMPROVISATION
POEM

How do we spread this bill?

You tap your pencil on a desk.

Naoko Fujimoto Dec. 2016

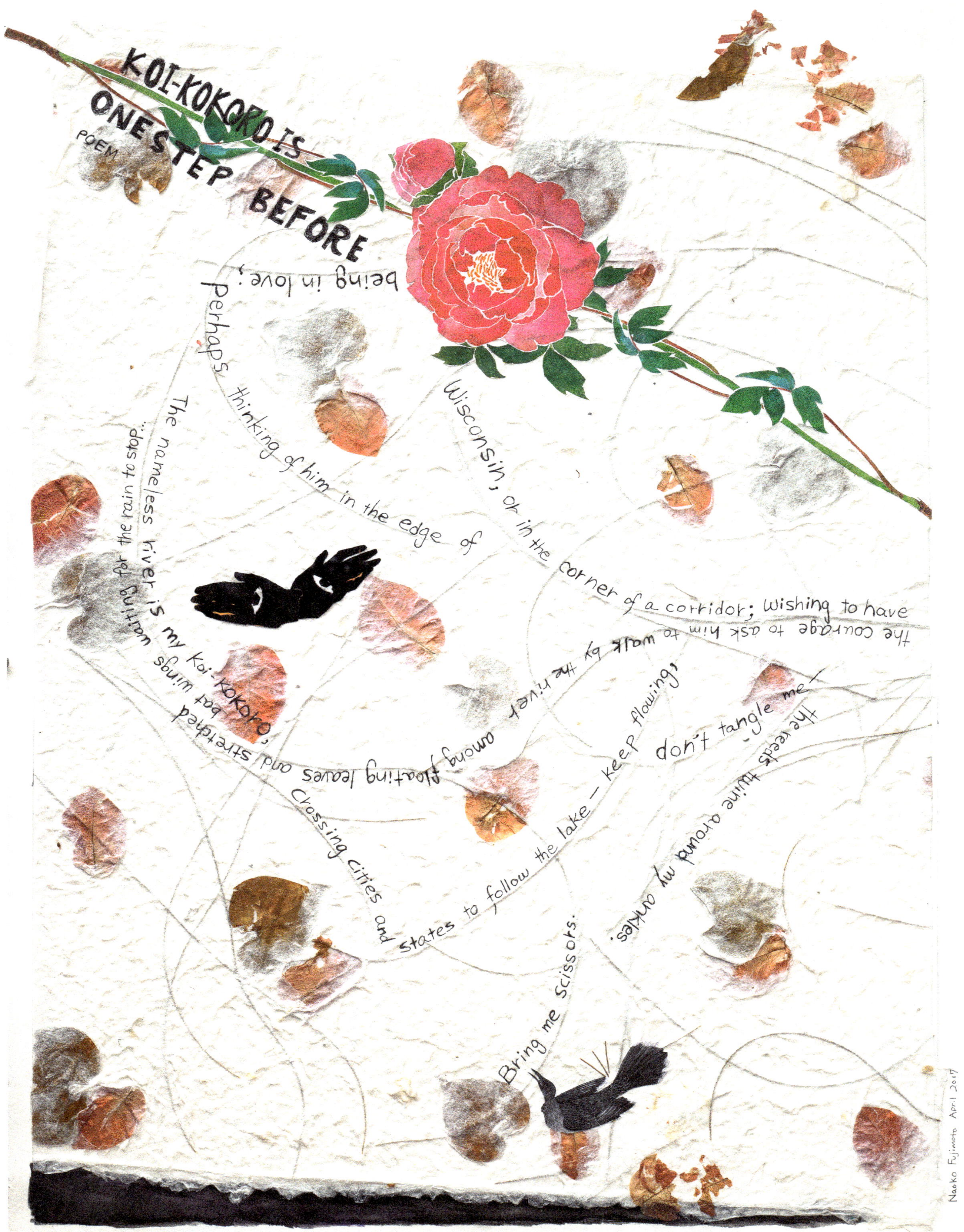

KOI-KOKORO IS ONE STEP BEFORE
POEM
being in love:
Perhaps, thinking of him in the edge of
Wisconsin, or in the corner of a corridor; wishing to have
the courage to ask him to walk by the river among floating leaves and stretched
bat wings — my Koi-kokoro,
The nameless river is my Koi-kokoro, but wings not stretched
praying for the rain to stop...
Crossing cities and states to follow the lake — keep flowing;
don't tangle me —
the reeds twine around my ankles;
Bring me scissors.
Naoko Fujimoto April 2017

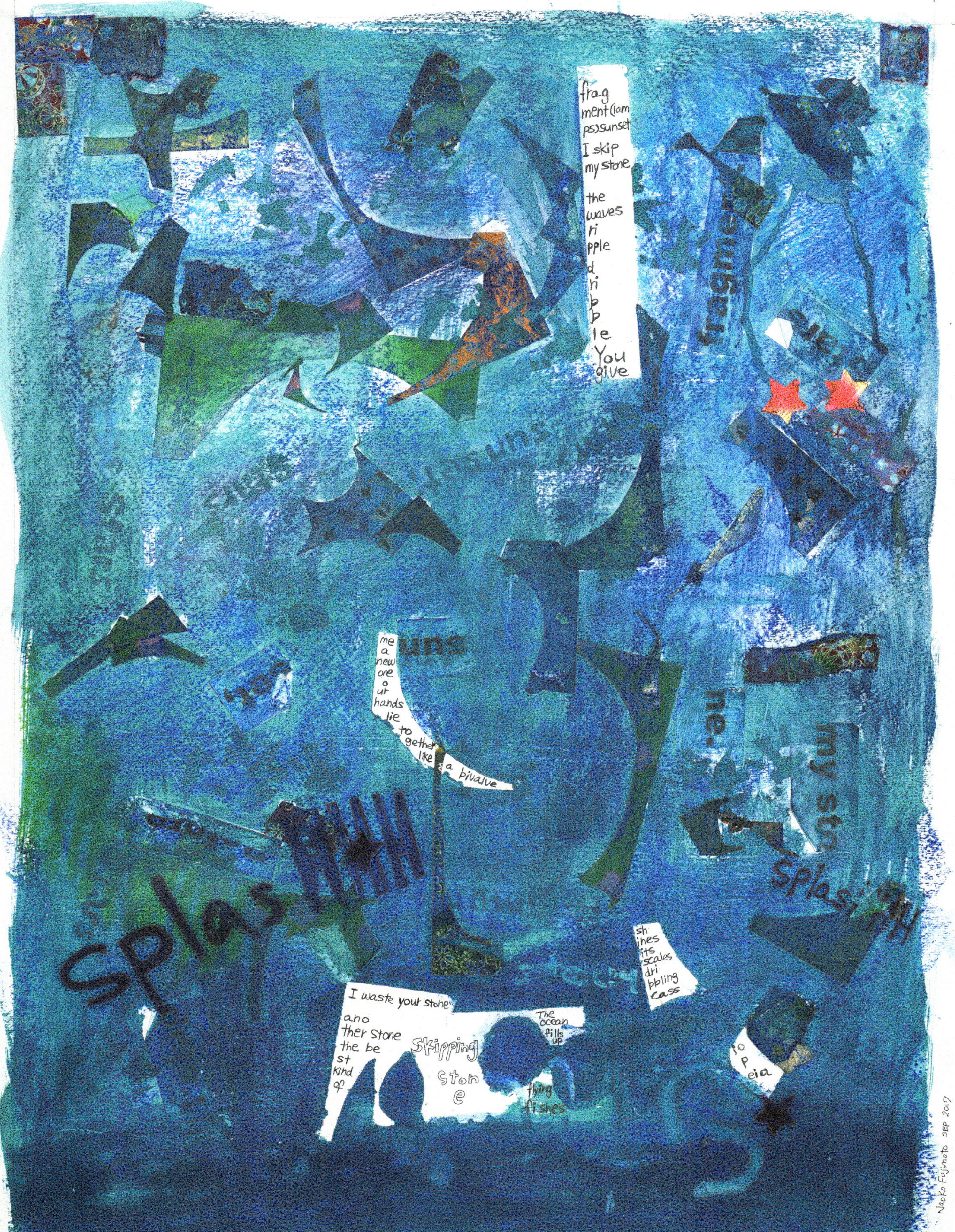

frag
ment (lam
ps) sunset
I skip
my stone
the
waves
ri
pple
d
ri
b
b
le
You
give
me
a
new
o
u
r
hands
lie
to
gether
like
a bivalve
fragment
my stone
I waste your stone
ano
ther stone
the be
st
kind
of
Skipping
Ston
e
The
ocean
fills up
Flying
fishes
sh
ines
its
scales
dri
bbling
cass
Splash
Splash
Naoko Fujimoto SEP 2017

to climb up to the NOVEMBER clouds.

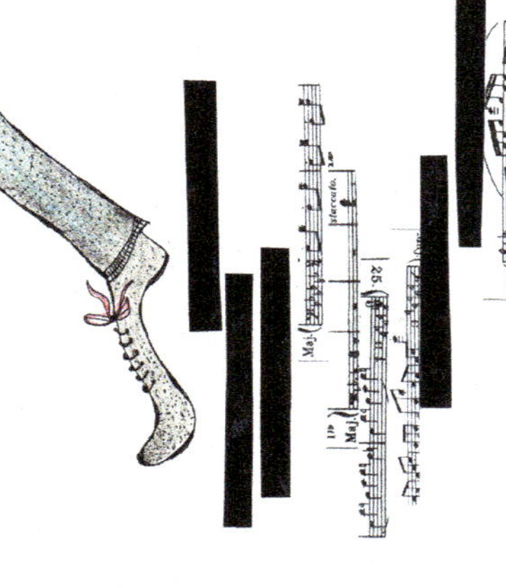

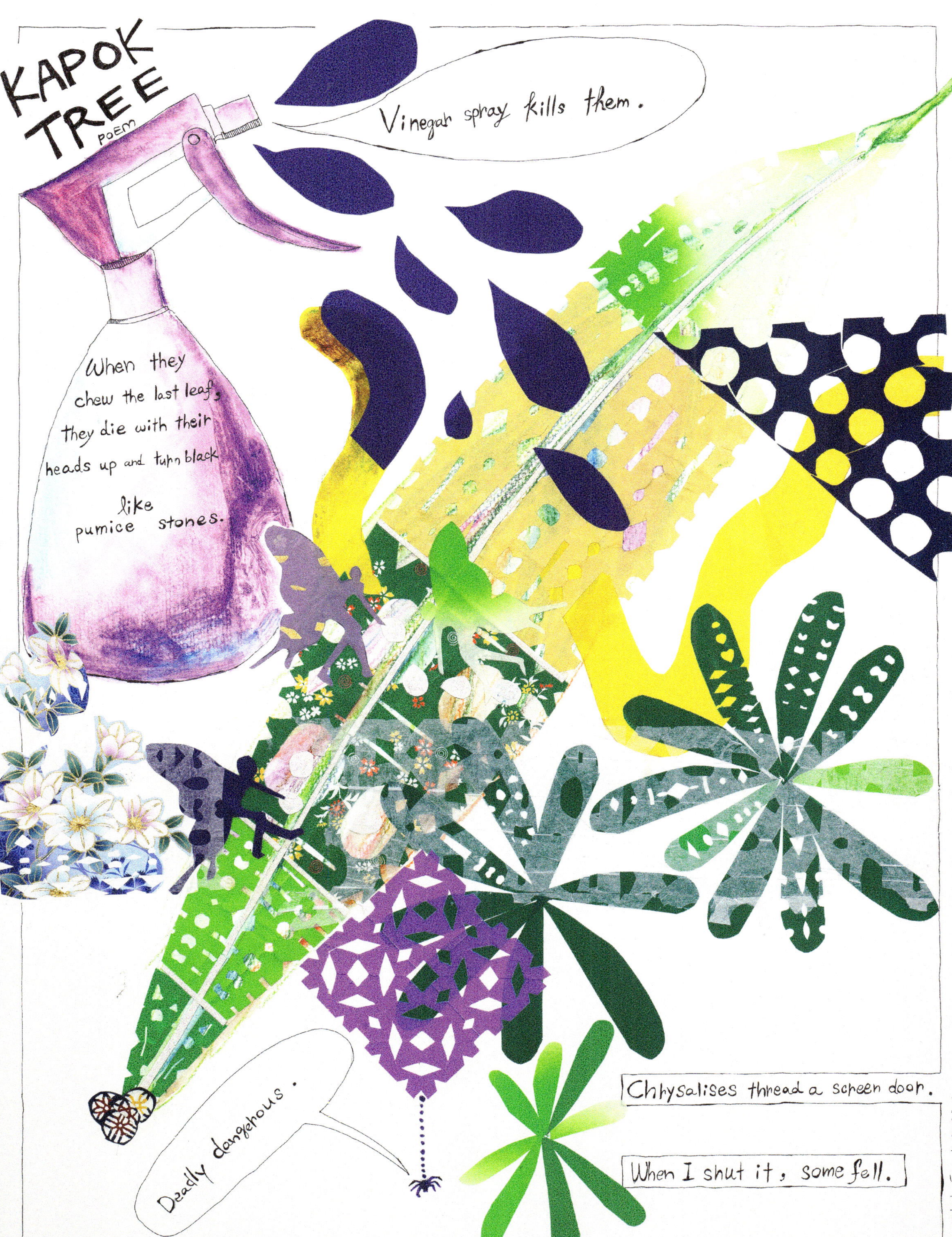

KAPOK TREE
POEM
Vinegar spray kills them.
When they
chew the last leaf,
they die with their
heads up and turn black
like
pumice stones.
Deadly dangerous .
Chrysalises thread a screen door.
When I shut it, some fell.
Naoko Fujimoto DEC 2016

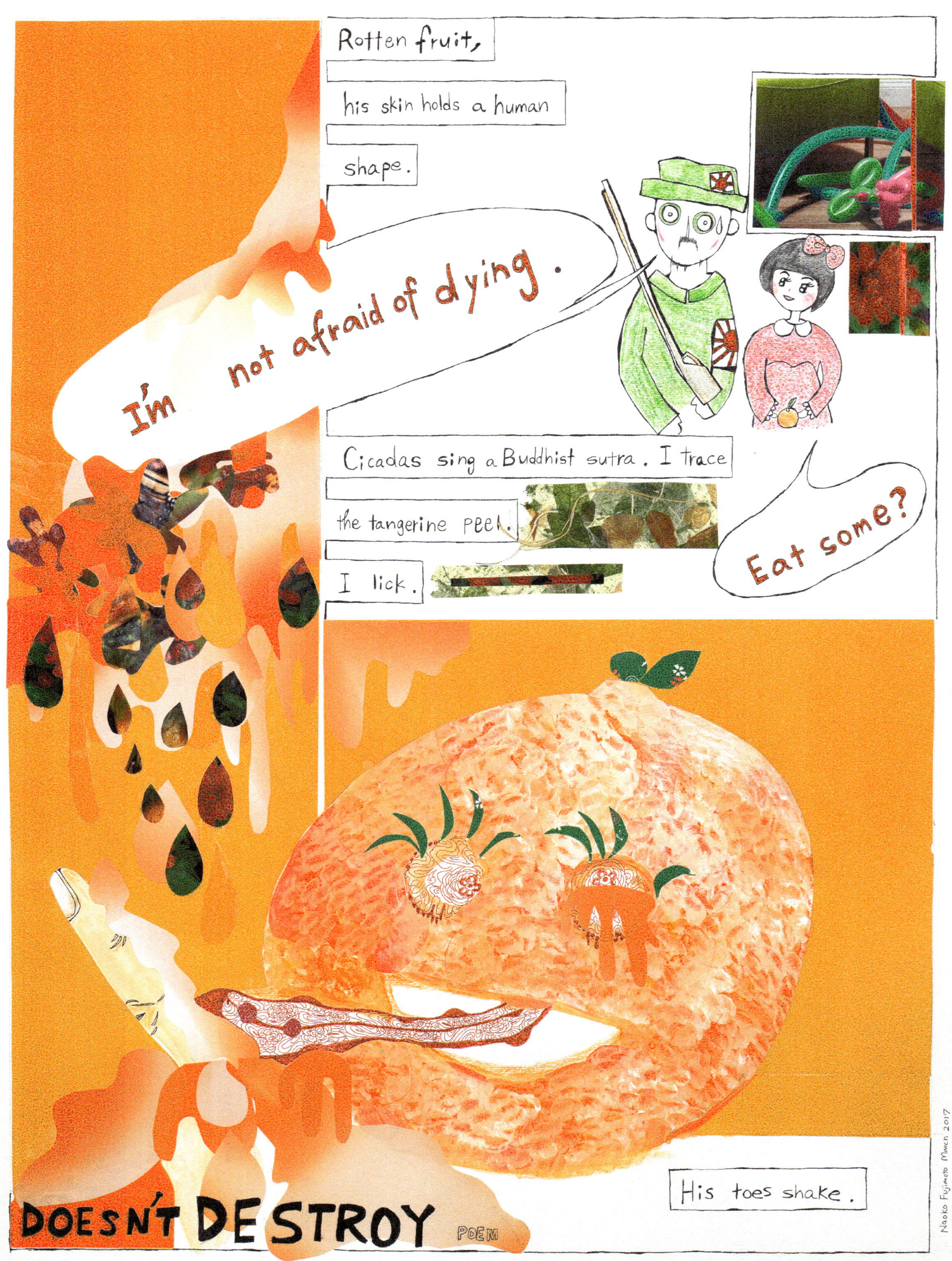

Rotten fruit,
his skin holds a human
shape.
I'm not afraid of dying.
Cicadas sing a Buddhist sutra. I trace
the tangerine peel.
I lick.
Eat some?
DOESN'T DESTROY
POEM
His toes shake.
Naoko Fujimoto Mexn 2017

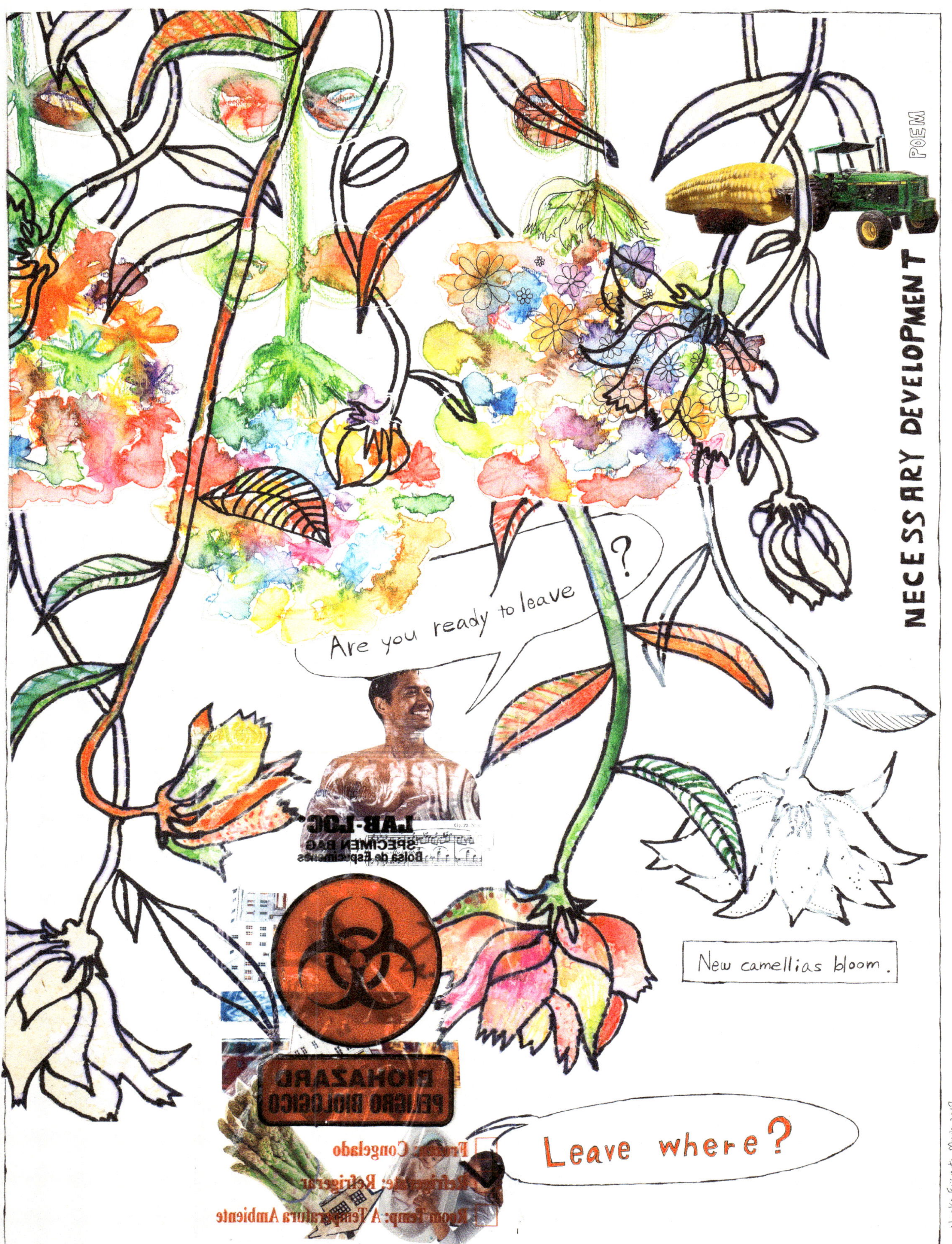
POEM
NECESSARY DEVELOPMENT
Are you ready to leave ?
New camellias bloom.
Leave where?
Naoko Fujimoto March 2017

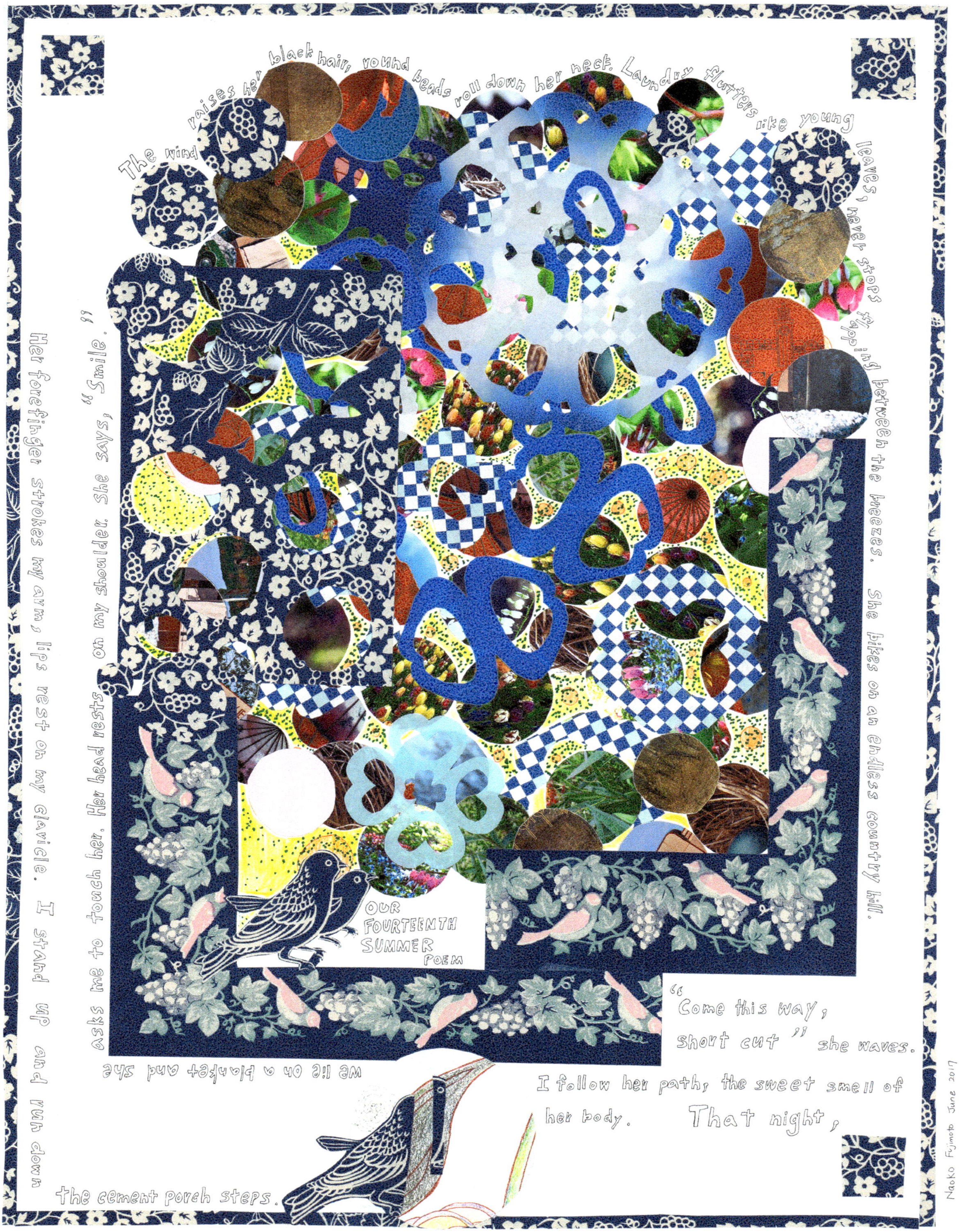

The wind raises her black hair, round beads roll down her neck. Laundry flutters like young leaves, never stops flapping between the breezes. She bikes on an endless country hill.

Her forefinger strokes my arm, lips rest on my clavicle. I stand up and run down the cement porch steps.

we lie on a blanket and she asks me to touch her. Her head rests on my shoulder, she says, "Smile."

OUR FOURTEENTH SUMMER POEM

"Come this way, short cut" she waves. I follow her path, the sweet smell of her body. That night,

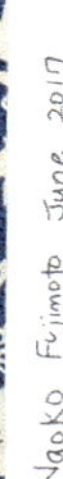

Naoko Fujimoto June 2017

NATANE RAIN IS
POEM
a glass of lemonade; unexpected sleet; gutters bubble, puddles reflect the magnolia trees, whose petals with other edges — frost bites — I am careful,
careful to
touch them, as if cleaning contact lens. You hide thin blue layers over brown irises under a wall of dragonfly eyeglasses.
Naoko Fujimoto MAY 2017

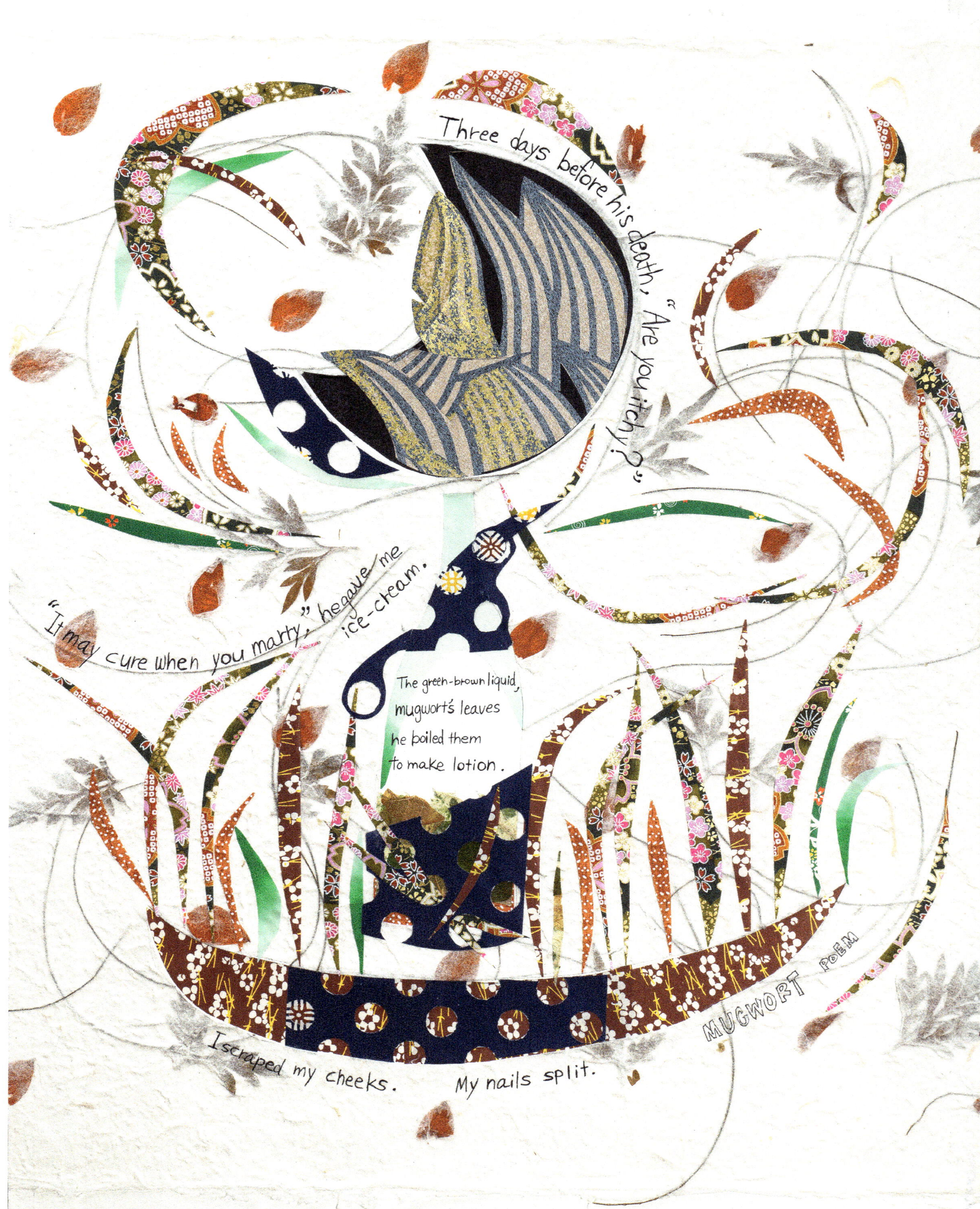
Three days before his death, "Are you itchy?"
"It may cure when you marry," he gave me ice-cream.
The green-brown liquid, mugwort's leaves he boiled them to make lotion.
I scraped my cheeks.
My nails split.
MUGWORT POEM
Naoko Fujimoto June 2017

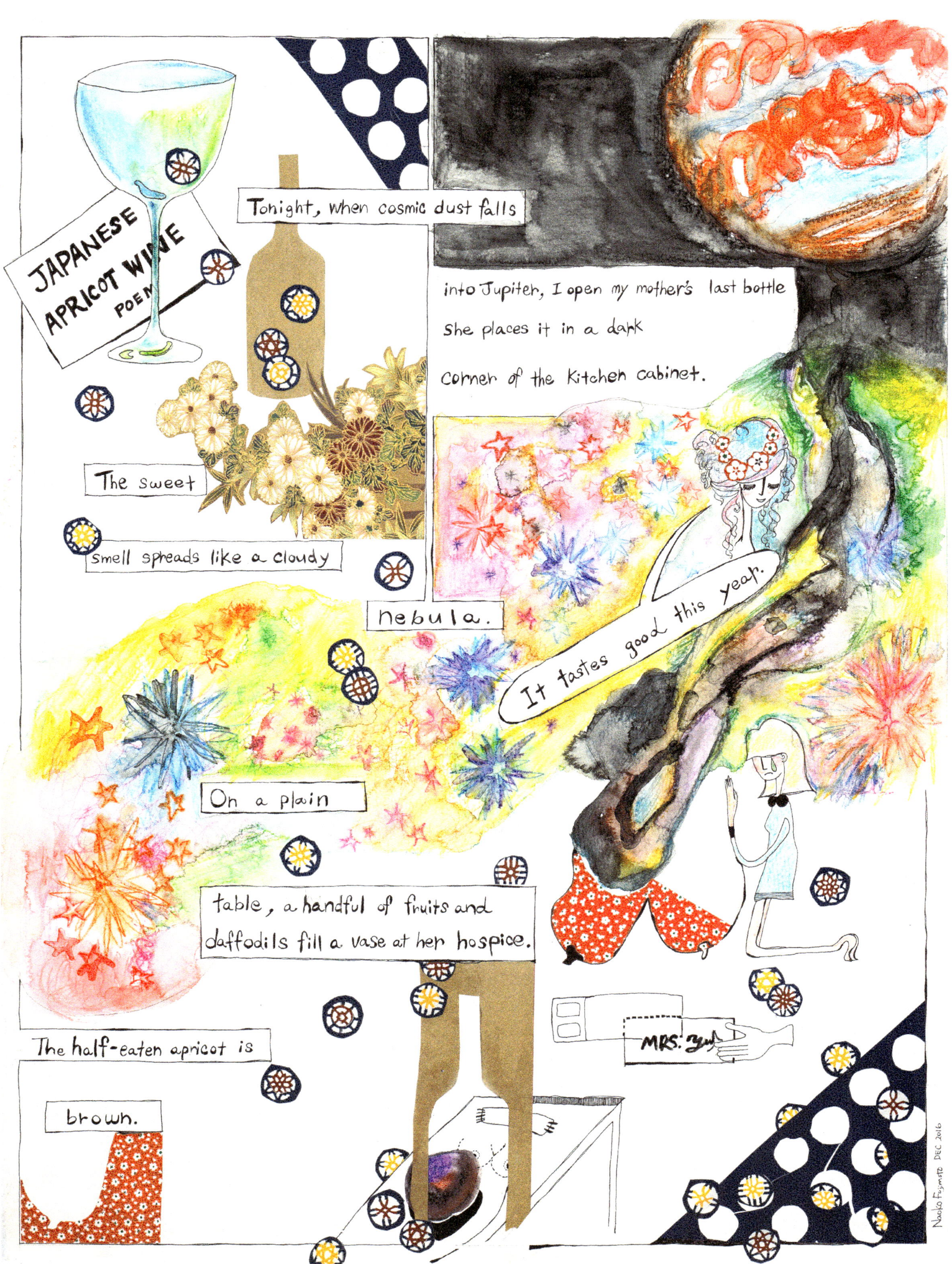

JAPANESE APRICOT WINE POEM
Tonight, when cosmic dust falls
into Jupiter, I open my mother's last bottle
She places it in a dark
corner of the kitchen cabinet.
The sweet
smell spreads like a cloudy
nebula.
It tastes good this year.
On a plain
table, a handful of fruits and
daffodils fill a vase at her hospice.
The half-eaten apricot is
brown.
MRS.

Smells her neck.

her arms, lost breasts.

THE PAY PHONE

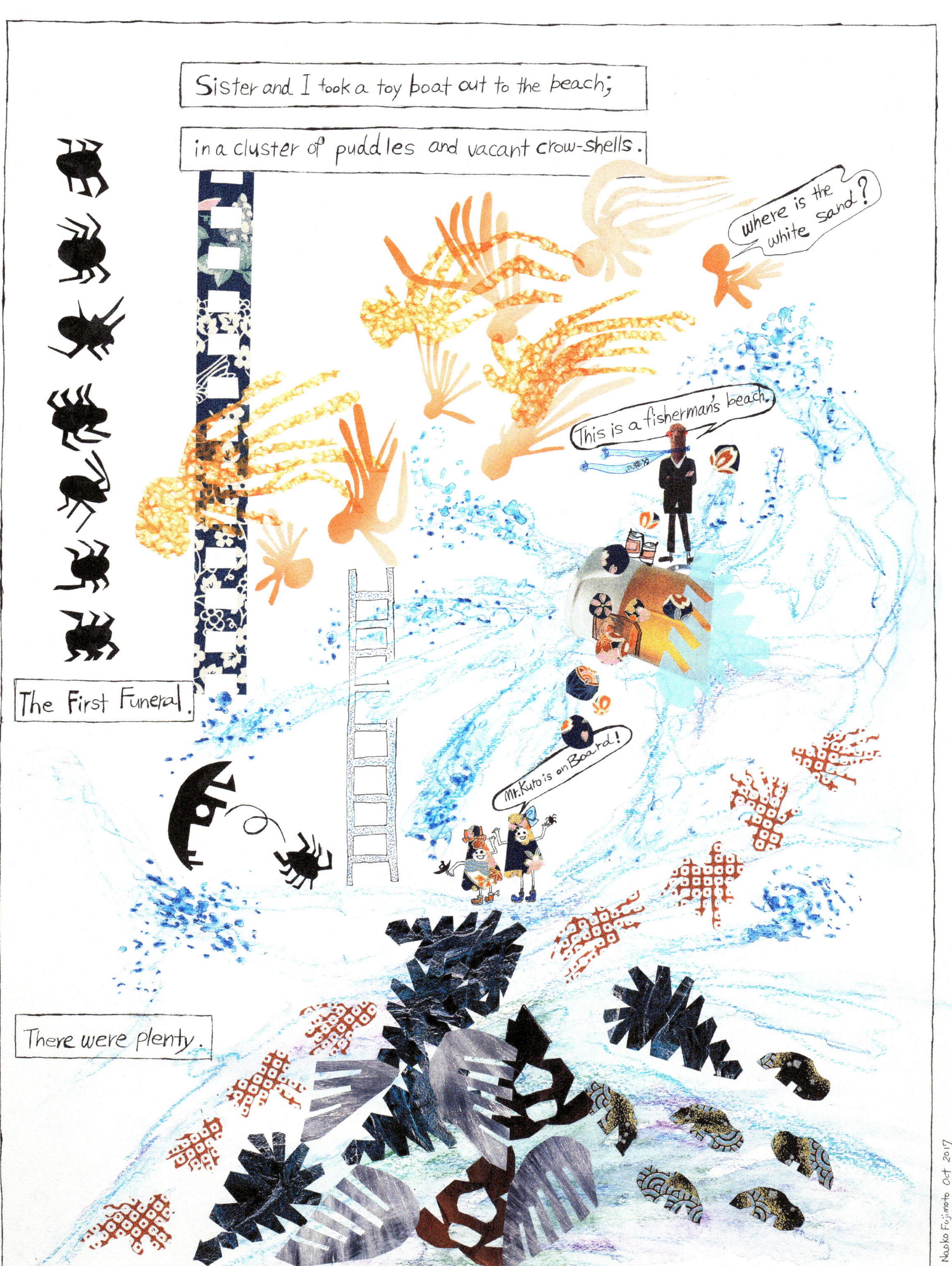

Sister and I took a toy boat out to the beach;
in a cluster of puddles and vacant crow-shells.
where is the white sand?
This is a fisherman's beach.
Mr. Kuto is on Board!
The First Funeral.
There were plenty.

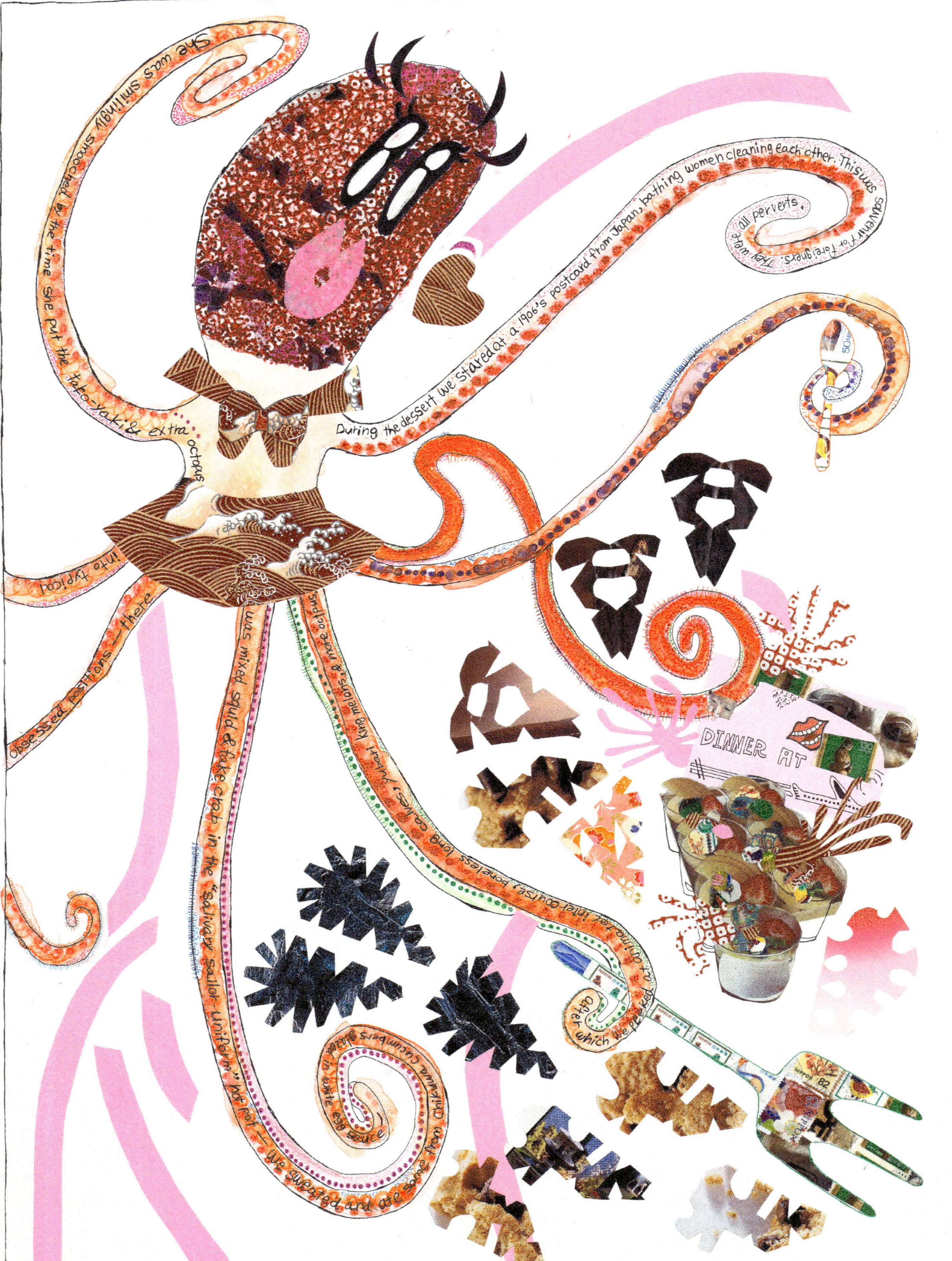

She was smilingly smooched by the time she put the takoyaki & extra octopus into typical obsessed positions —there
was mixed squid & fake crab in the "salivary sailor-uniform" hot pot — we slurped and ate some from Chikuwa and cucumbers stuck in white egg sauce
During the dessert we stared at a 1906's postcard from Japan, bathing women cleaning each other. This was a souvenir for foreigners. They were all perverts.
a whole octopus buried alive, boneless, long calves, inter course, pouring after which we peeked at
DINNER AT
Naoko Fujimoto SEP 2017

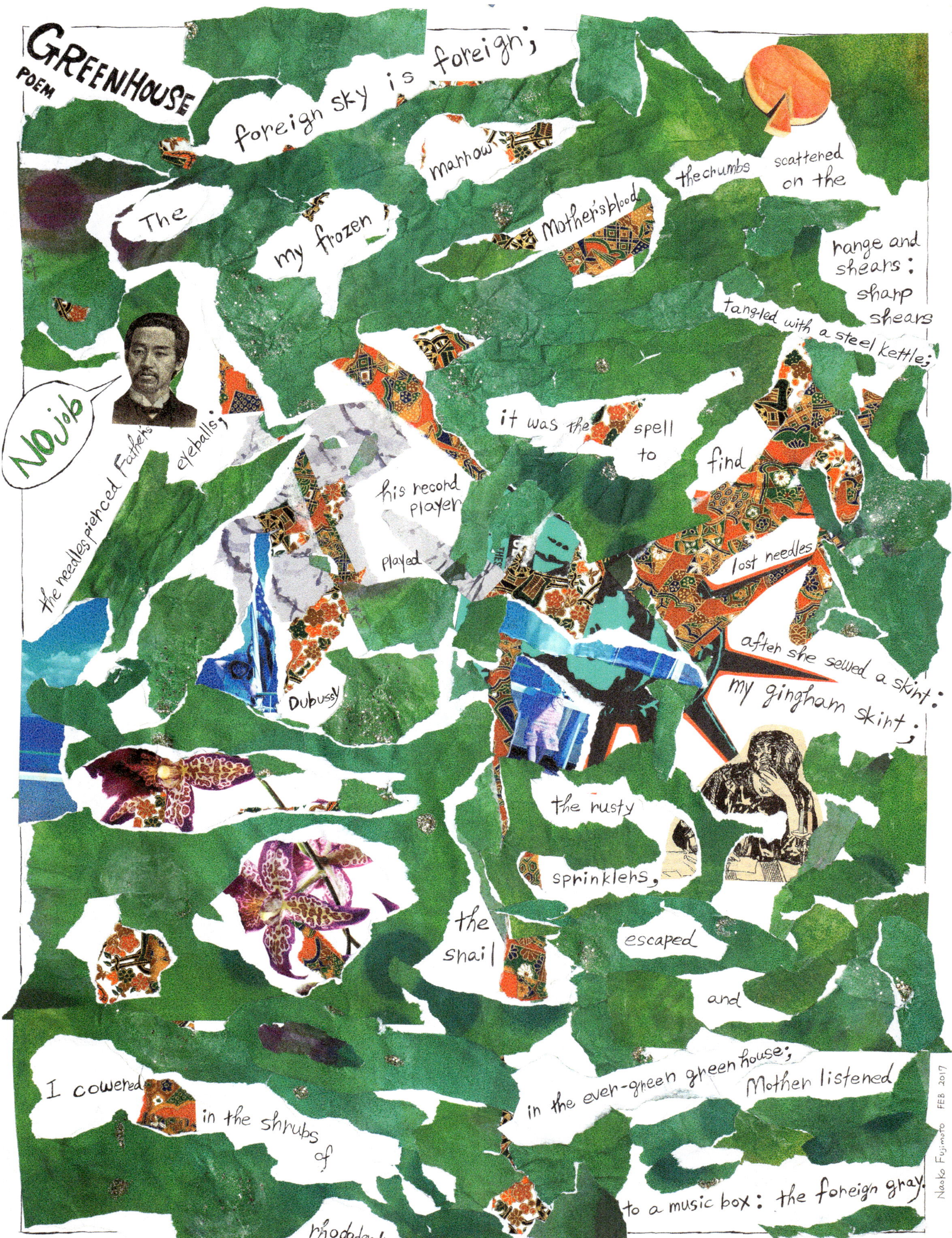

GREENHOUSE
POEM
The foreign sky is foreign;
my frozen marrow
Mother's blood the chumbs scattered on the
range and shears: sharp shears
tangled with a steel kettle;
it was the spell to find
NO job
the needles pierced Father's eyeballs;
his record player
played
Dubussy
lost needles
after she sewed a skirt:
my gingham skirt;
the rusty
sprinklers,
the snail escaped
and
I cowered in the shrubs of
in the ever-green greenhouse; Mother listened
to a music box : the foreign gray.
rhododendron;
Naoko Fujimoto FEB 2017

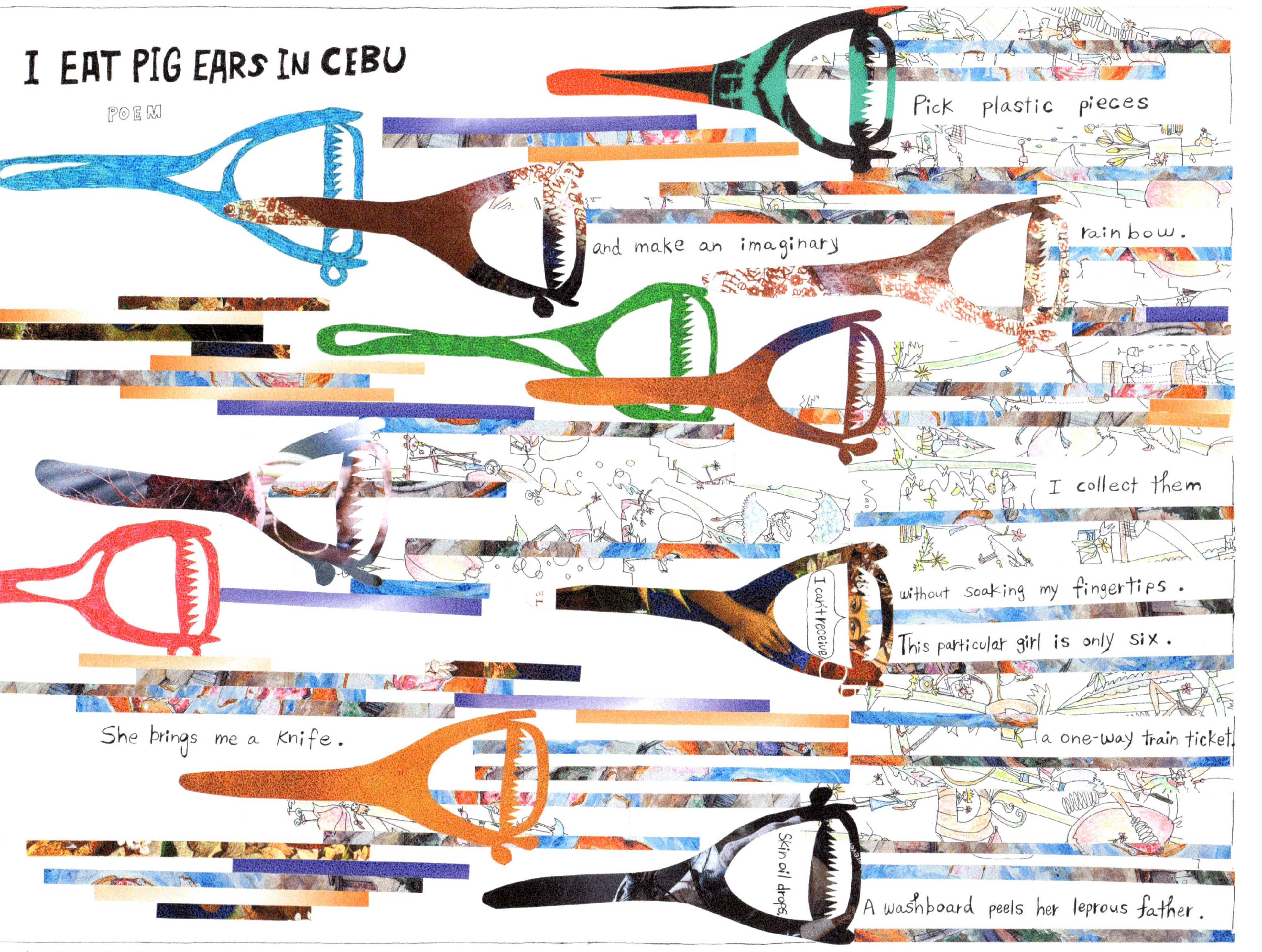

I EAT PIG EARS IN CEBU
POEM
Pick plastic pieces
and make an imaginary
rainbow.
I collect them
without soaking my fingertips.
This particular girl is only six.
I can't receive
a one-way train ticket.
She brings me a knife.
Skin oil drops.
A washboard peels her leprous father.
Naoko Fujimoto FER 2017

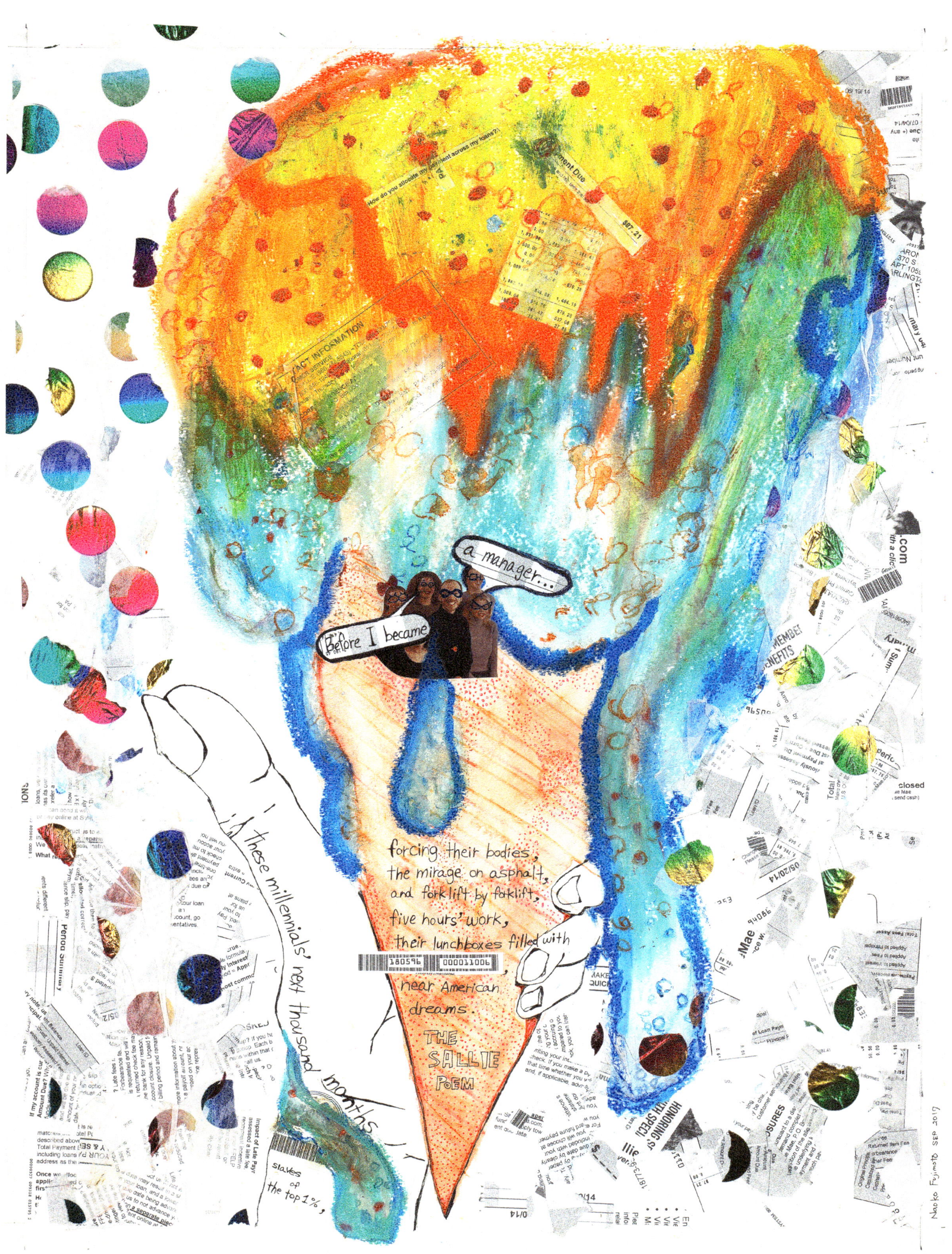
a manager...
Before I became
forcing their bodies,
the mirage on asphalt,
and forklift by forklift,
five hours' work,
their lunchboxes filled with
near American
dreams.
THE
SALLIE
POEM
these millennials' next thousand months
slaves of
the top 1%
Naoko Fujimoto SEP 2017

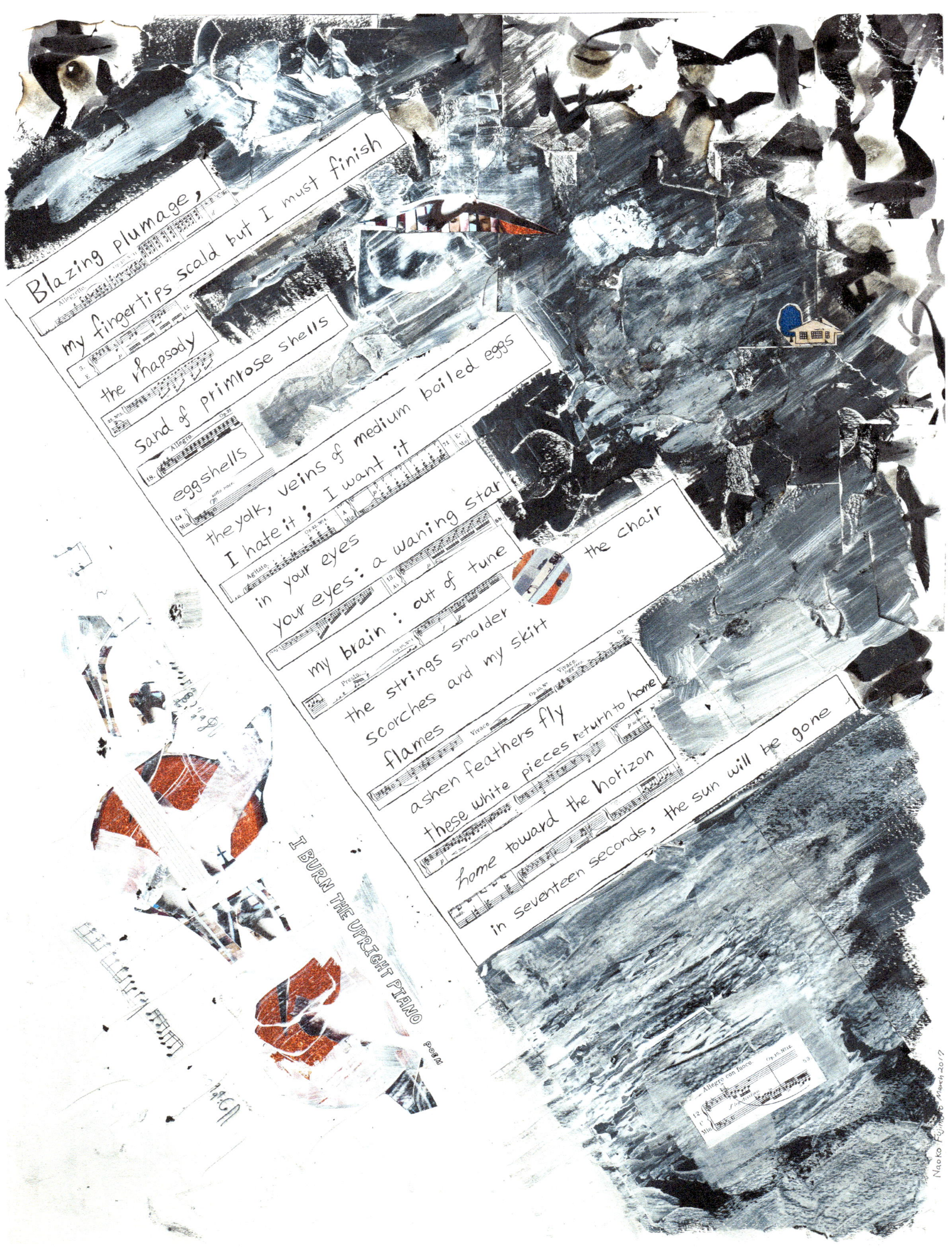

Blazing plumage,
my fingertips scald but I must finish
the rhapsody
sand of primrose shells
eggshells
the yolk, veins of medium boiled eggs
I hate it ; I want it
in your eyes
your eyes : a waning star
my brain : out of tune
the chair
the strings smolder
scorches and my skirt
flames
ashen feathers fly
these white pieces return to home
home toward the horizon
in seventeen seconds, the sun will be gone
I BURN THE UPRIGHT PIANO
poem
Naoko Fujimoto March 2017

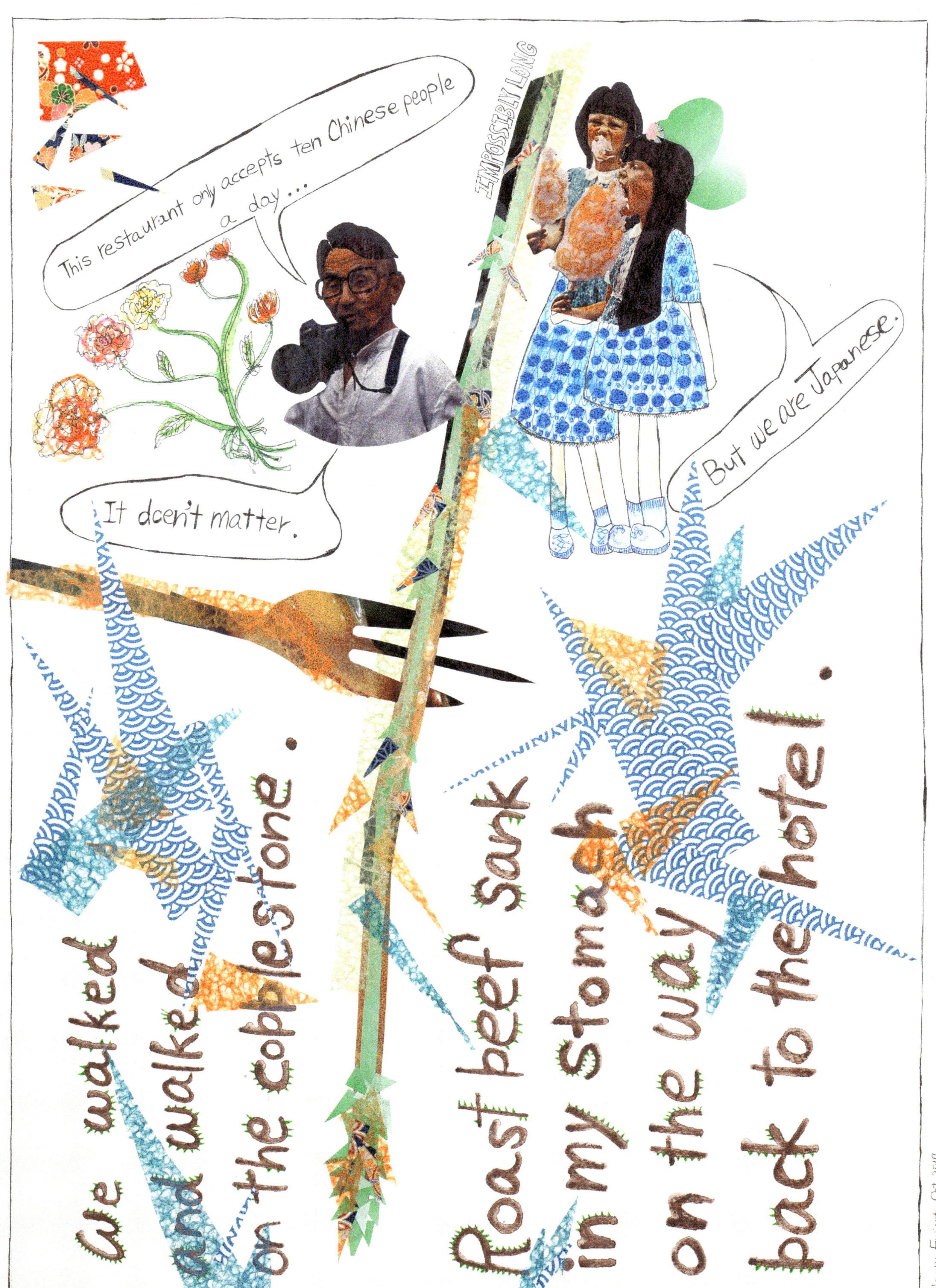

This restaurant only accepts ten Chinese people a day ...
It doesn't matter.
IMPOSSIBLY LONG
But we are Japanese.
We walked and walked on the cobblestone.
Roast beef sank in my stomach on the way back to the hotel.
Naoko Fujimoto Oct 2017

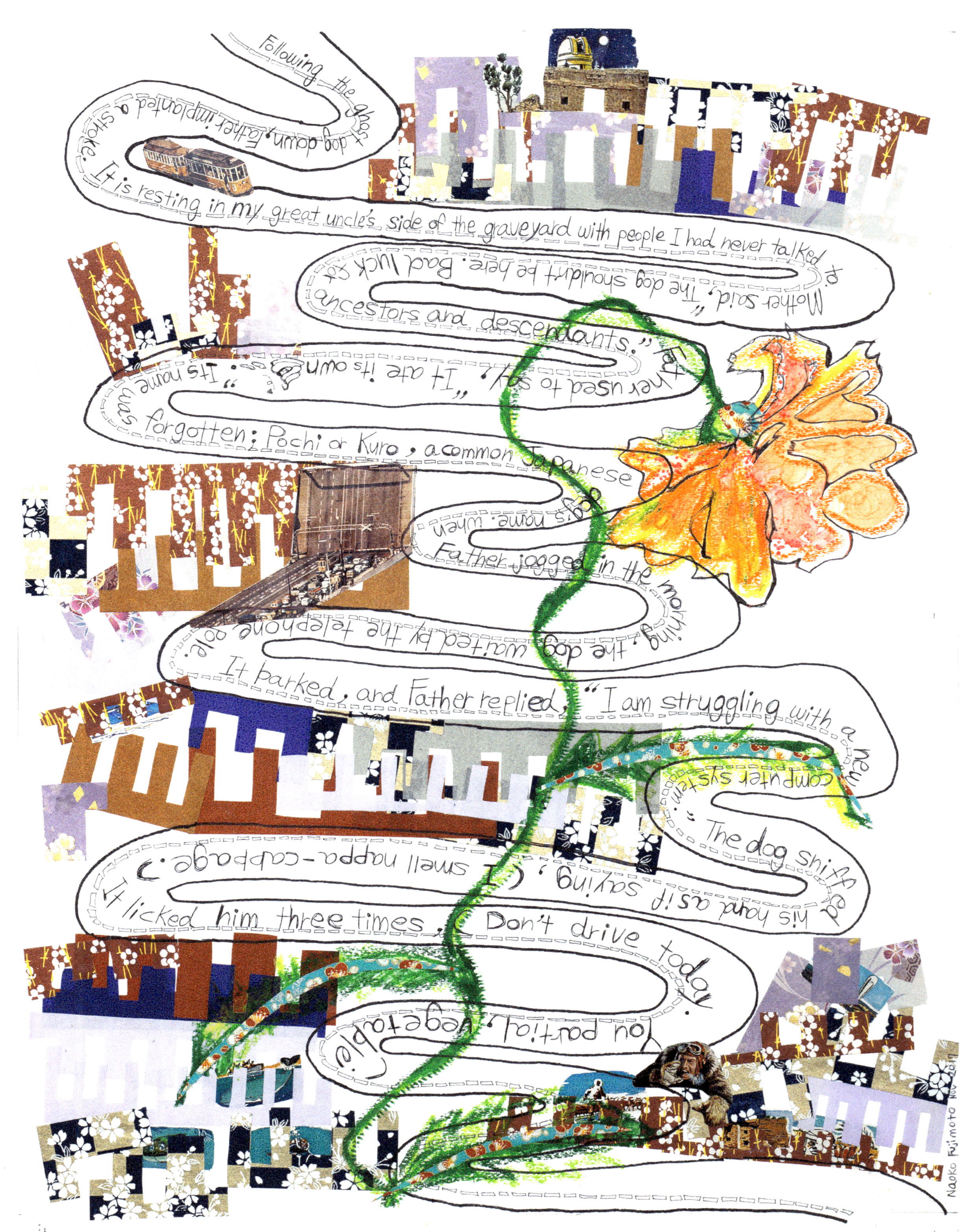

Following the ghost dog down, Father implanted a stroke.
It is resting in my great uncle's side of the graveyard with people I had never talked to.
Mother said, "The dog shouldn't be here. Bad luck for ancestors and descendants."
Father used to say, "It ate its own." "Its name was forgotten: Pochi or Kuro, a common Japanese dog's name." When Father jogged in the morning, the dog ran from the woods waited by the telephone pole.
It barked, and Father replied, "I am struggling with a new computer system." The dog shifted his body as if saying, "Don't drive today. You partial vegetable." It licked him three times. "I smell nappa-cabbage."
Naoko Fujimoto Nov 2018

I slough off your blanket; your   pubic hair: my lost

long hair; my toe dampens in a   muddled rut;
snow: soundless snowflake,   falls; I wear
mourning; a cloud flows in vacancy:

the vacant moon: no headlights   I carry my lithograph;
the plastic lithograph glued   with a half-eaten rotten

tomato; I die; no spring   clod;
sleet hisses on my skin when   the first
    falls on my nape:
acid rain: oval mauve acid,
the smallest vermeil bud opens;   I'm a marionette; his
wrist: his artery: the warmest artery of his forefinger;
my thigh; his   pulse: it is spring; the warmest   spring
foot prints of deer   are on the snow hut; I'm naked;   the   naked
heat: rotten tomatoes under the white blanket.

WHITE
AVENUE
POEM

Naoko Fujimoto FEB 2017

my toe nails are wet too
the dew drops spread
over the highest pine tree
like lanterns between nets
glimmering under the canopy
and it takes a while to realize
they are lightning bugs
branching out. Fluttering lightly.
I am speachless beside you.   For you,
this is a normal sunset behind your backyard
by a street where Native Americans used to run
with thir hair streaming in the wind.
It's path guides all living creatures   raccoons,
birds, grasshoppers,   and us;
nothing entwined
stretching out to the moon   like a ballon
rising until it disappears.
I say,
"thank you"
you nearly hear me.

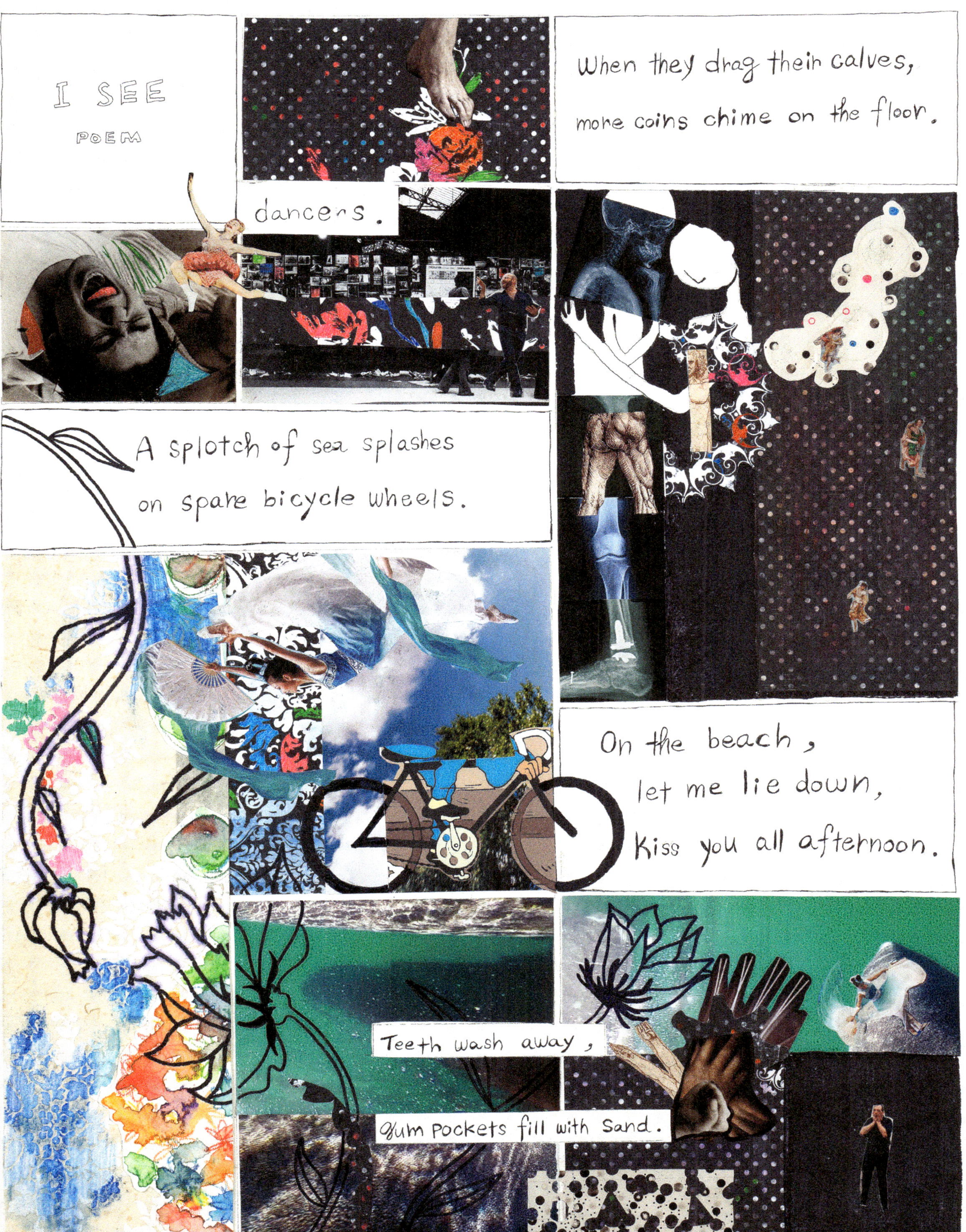

I SEE
POEM

When they drag their calves,
more coins chime on the floor.

dancers.

A splotch of sea splashes
on spare bicycle wheels.

On the beach,
let me lie down,
kiss you all afternoon.

Teeth wash away,

gum pockets fill with sand.

Naoko Fujimoto Jan 2017

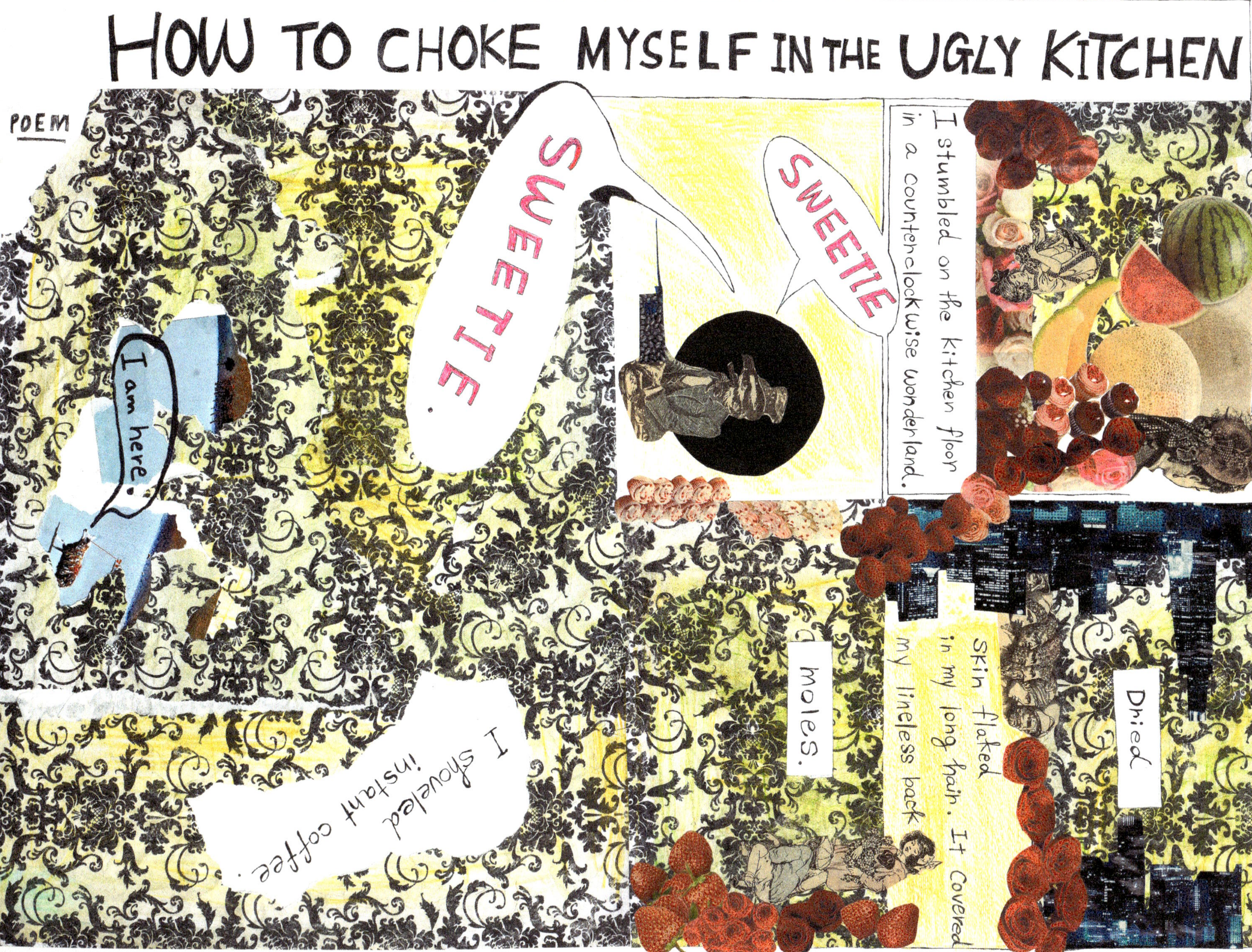

HOW TO CHOKE MYSELF IN THE UGLY KITCHEN
POEM
SWEETIE
SWEETIE
I am here.
I stumbled on the kitchen floor in a counterclockwise wonderland.
I shoveled instant coffee.
moles.
Skin flaked in my long hair. It covered my lineless back
Dried
Naoko Fujimoto Feb 2017

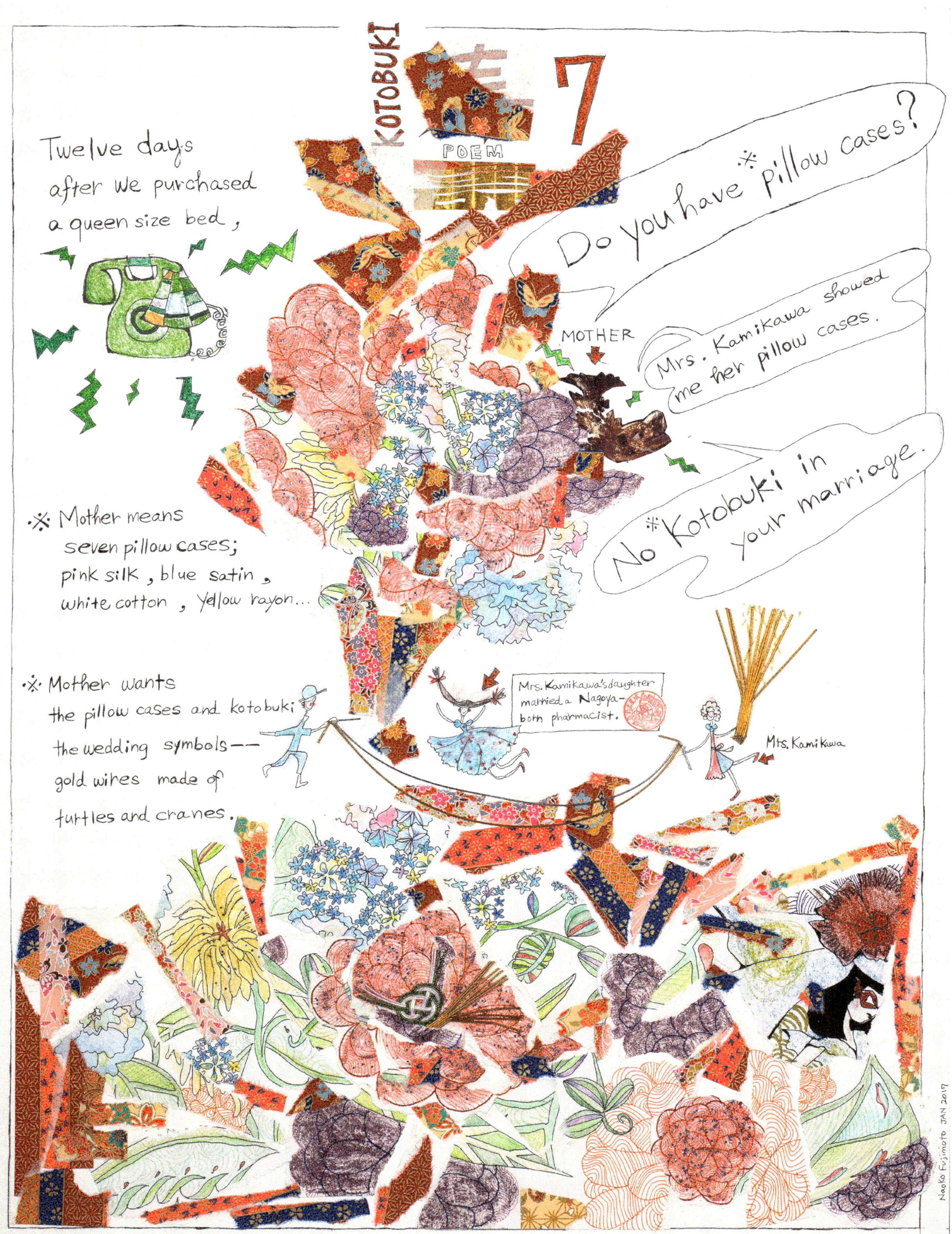

KOTOBUKI
POEM
7
Twelve days
after we purchased
a queen size bed,
Do you have ※ pillow cases?
MOTHER
Mrs. Kamikawa showed
me her pillow cases.
No ※ Kotobuki in
your marriage.
※ Mother means
seven pillow cases;
pink silk, blue satin,
white cotton, yellow rayon...
※ Mother wants
the pillow cases and kotobuki
the wedding symbols —
gold wires made of
turtles and cranes.
Mrs. Kamikawa's daughter
married a Nagoya-
born pharmacist.
Mrs. Kamikawa
Naoko Fujimoto JAN 2017

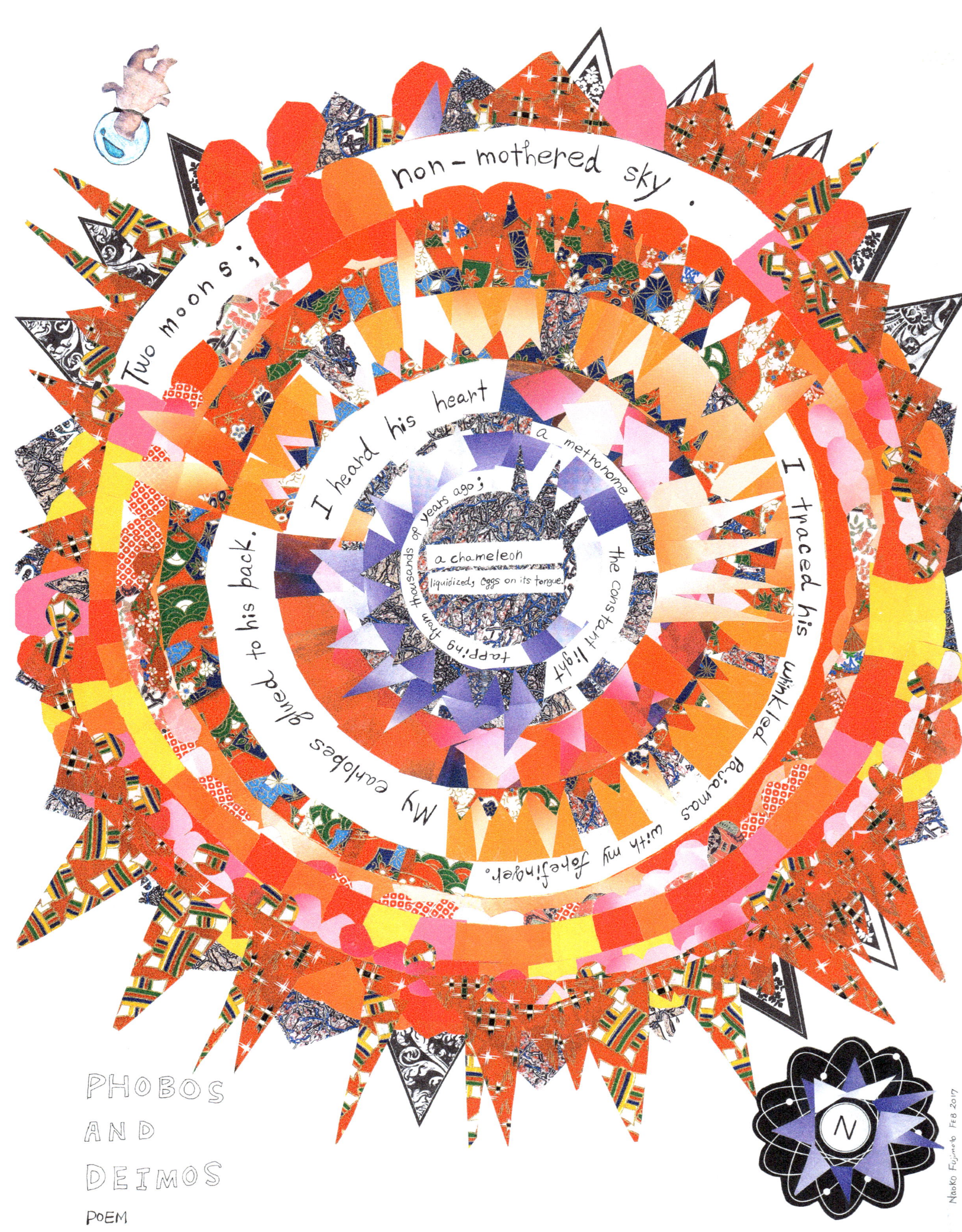

non - mothered sky .
Two moons;
I heard his heart
a metronome
of years ago;
a chameleon
liquidized eggs on its tongue.
tapping thousands
the constant light
I traced his wrinkled
with my forefinger.
My earlobes glued to his back.
Rejoicemos
PHOBOS AND DEIMOS
POEM
Naoko Fujimoto Feb 2017
N

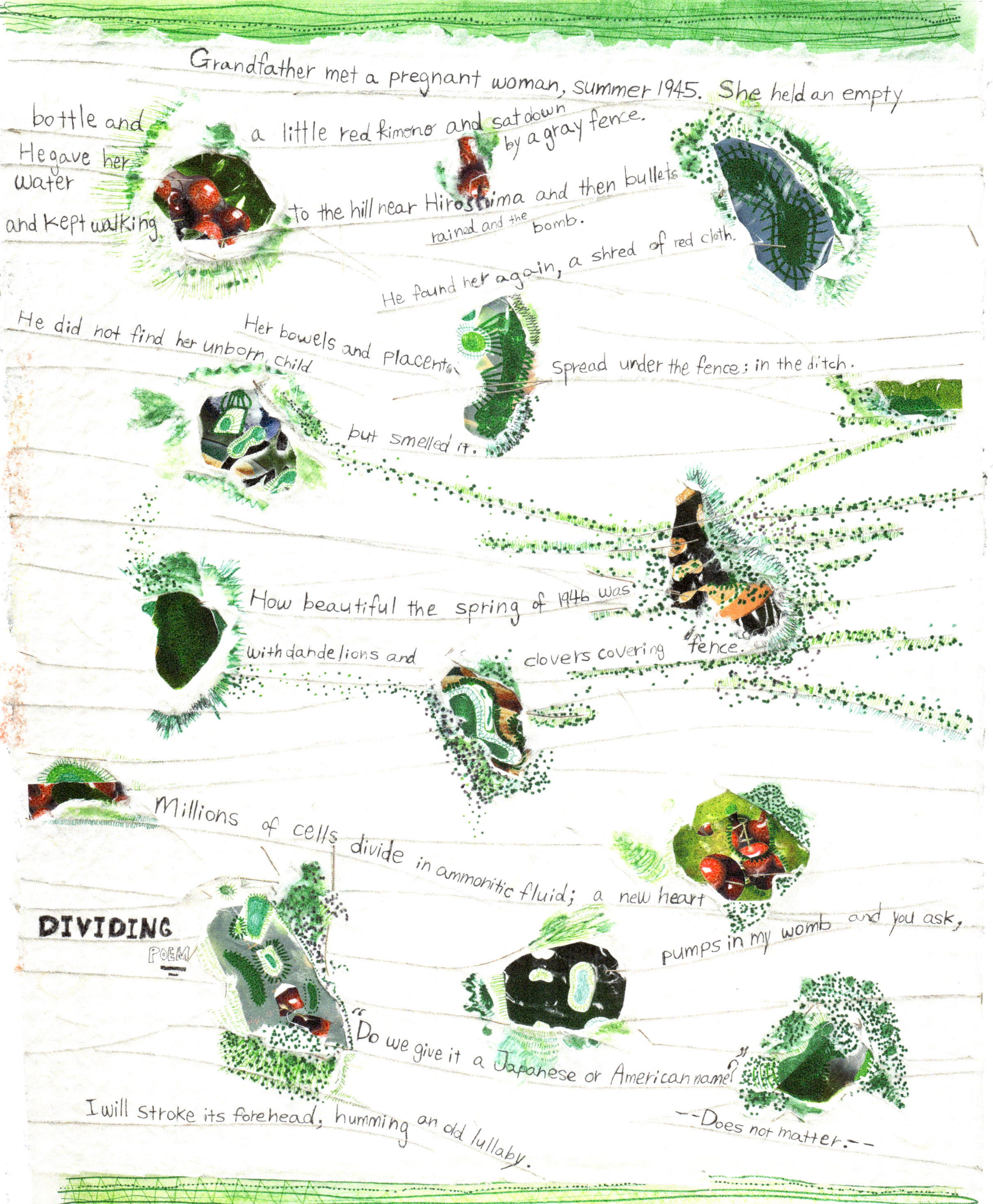

Grandfather met a pregnant woman, summer 1945. She held an empty
bottle and
a little red kimono and sat down
by a gray fence.
He gave her
water
and kept walking
to the hill near Hiroshima and then bullets
rained and the
bomb.
He found her again, a shred of red cloth.
He did not find her unborn child
Her bowels and placenta
Spread under the fence; in the ditch.
but smelled it.
How beautiful the spring of 1946 was
with dandelions and
clovers covering fence.
Millions of cells divide in ammonitic fluid; a new heart
DIVIDING
POEM
pumps in my womb and you ask,
"Do we give it a Japanese or American name?"
I will stroke its forehead, humming an old lullaby.
--Does not matter.--
Naoko Fujimoto MAY 2017

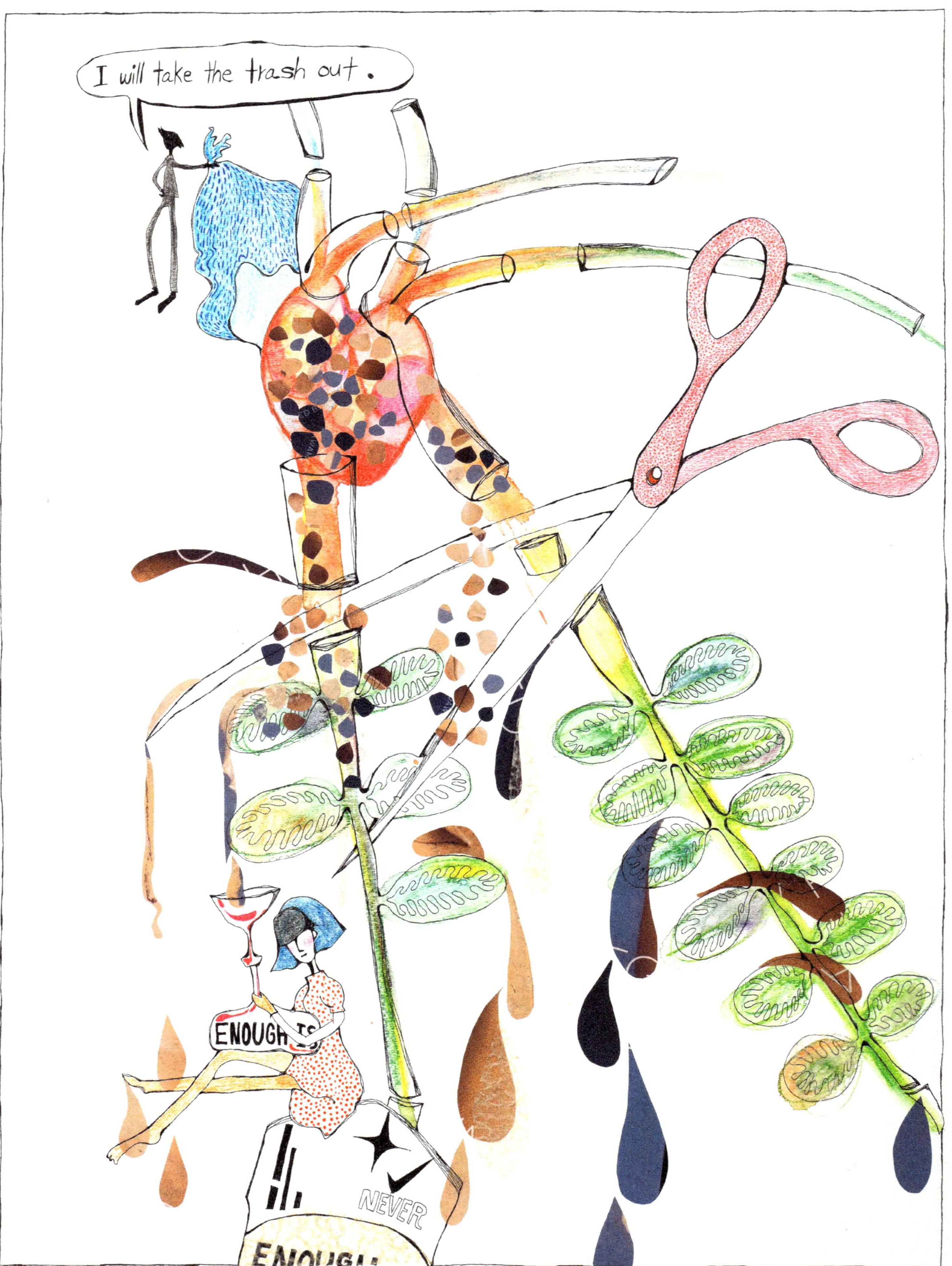

I will take the trash out.
ENOUGH IS
NEVER
ENOUGH
Naoko Fujimoto Dec 2017

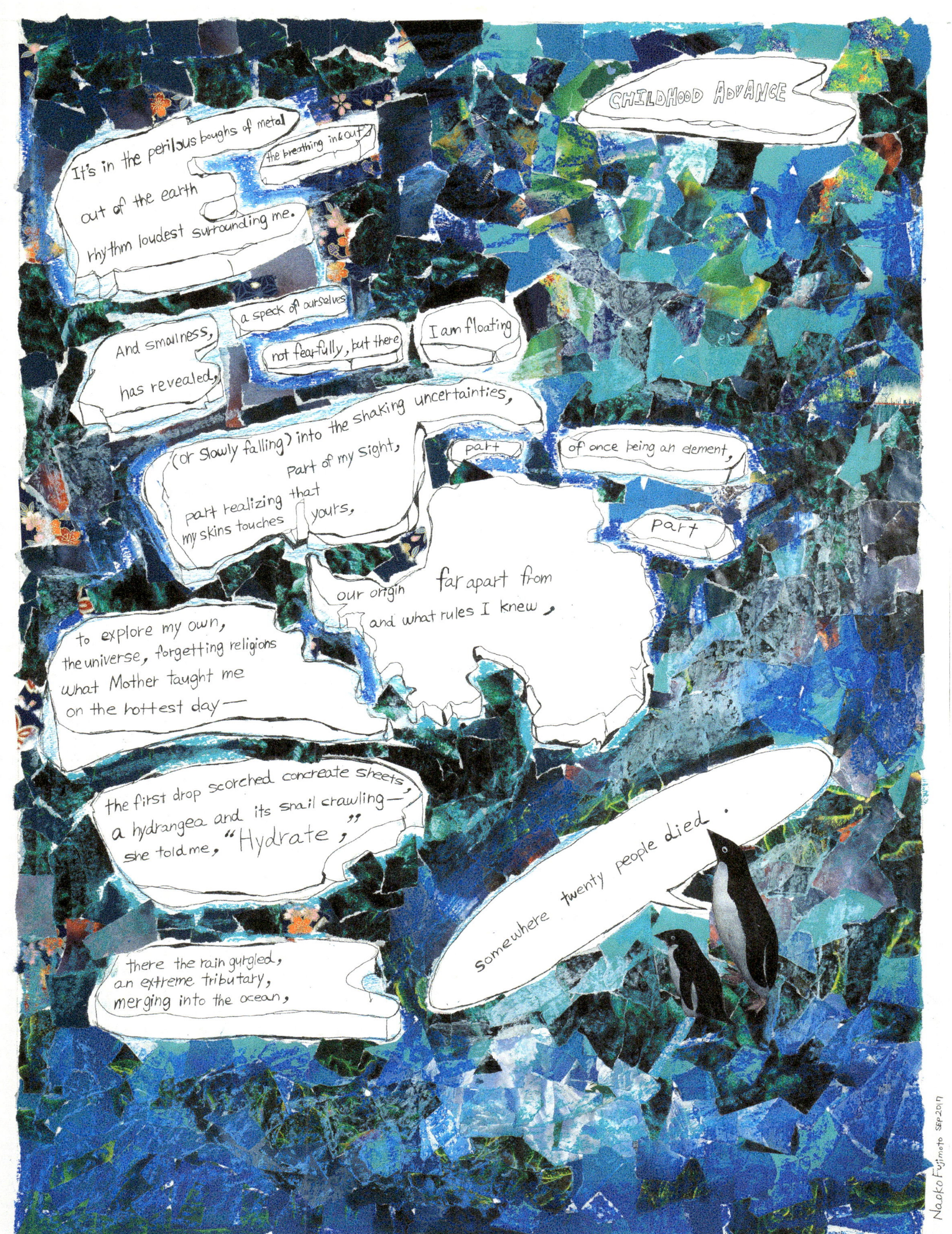

CHILDHOOD ADVANCE
It's in the perilous boughs of metal
the breathing in & out
out of the earth
rhythm loudest surrounding me.
And smallness,
a speck of ourselves
not fearfully, but there
I am floating
has revealed,
(or slowly falling) into the shaking uncertainties,
Part of my sight,
part
of once being an element,
part realizing that
my skins touches
yours,
part
our origin
far apart from
and what rules I knew ,
to explore my own,
the universe, forgetting religions
what Mother taught me
on the hottest day —
the first drop scorched concreate sheets,
a hydrangea and its snail crawling —
she told me, "Hydrate",
somewhere twenty people died .
there the rain gurgled,
an extreme tributary,
merging into the ocean,
Naoko Fujimoto SEP 2017

No clam's bubbles to stop on the lake beach.
Waves just come and go— no seaweed,
no fisherman's nets.

Plastic caps tumble,
but no head coral.
Lifeguard's freckled shoulders. Nobody screams, "Jellyfish!"
Wind tosses my hair across my mouth. I taste
nothing like standing by the seashore near your house— rusted
roots.

LAKE MICHIGAN

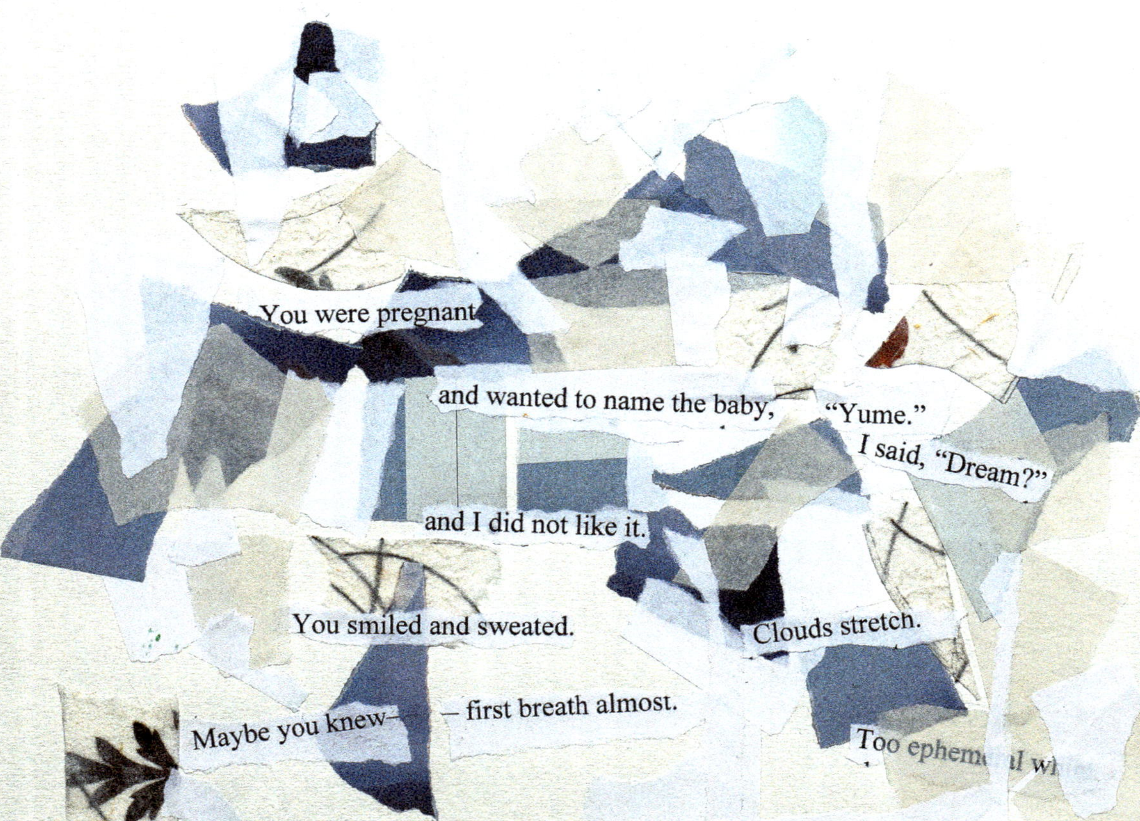

Naoko Fujimoto Oct 2017

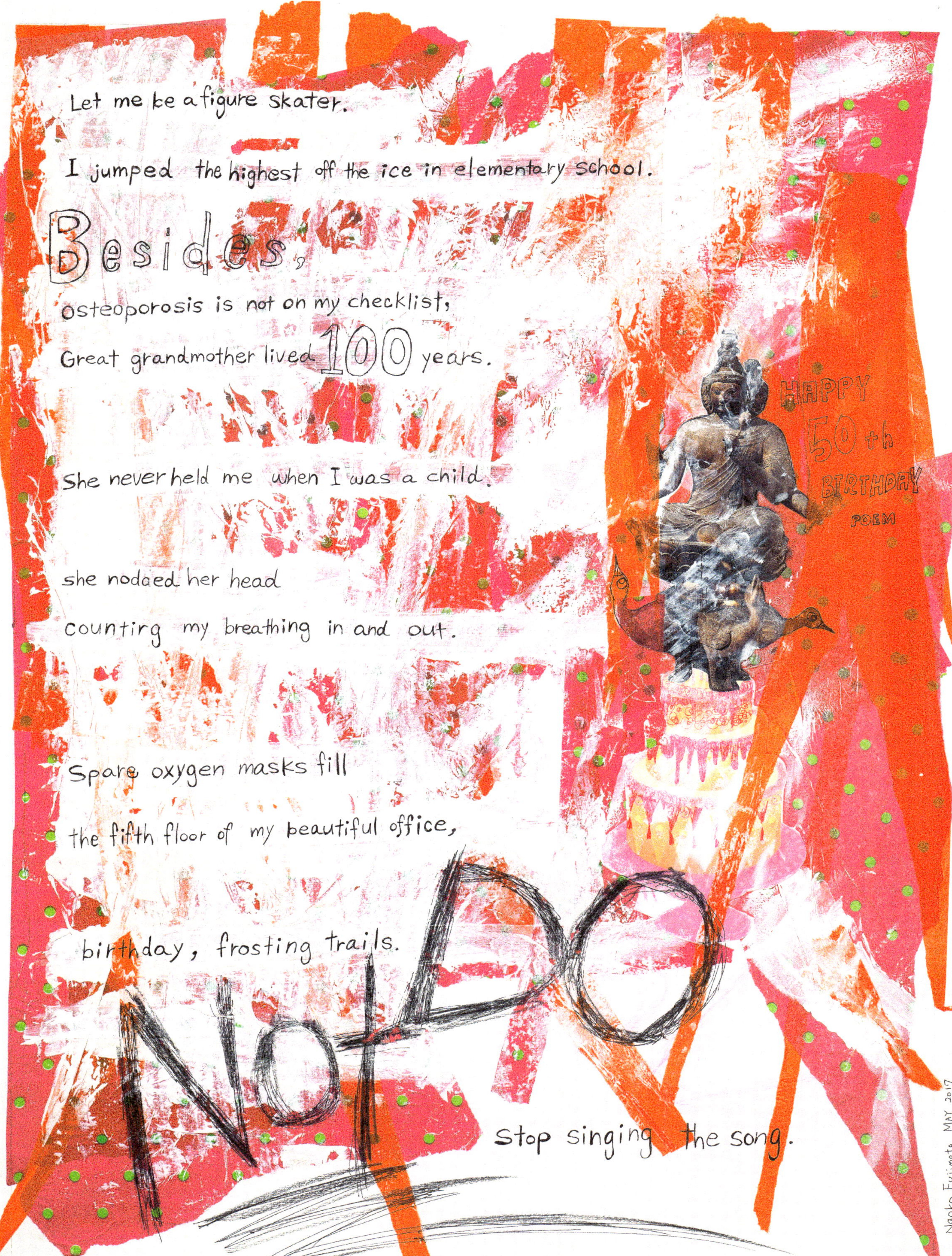

Let me be a figure skater.

I jumped the highest off the ice in elementary school.

Besides,

osteoporosis is not on my checklist;

Great grandmother lived 100 years.

She never held me when I was a child.

she nodded her head

counting my breathing in and out.

Spare oxygen masks fill

the fifth floor of my beautiful office,

birthday, frosting trails.

Not DO

Stop singing the song.

HAPPY 50th BIRTHDAY POEM

Naoko Fujimoto MAY 2017

Because there is no answer
beetles roll,
ants dismantle.

An ideal Summer
Shines more than fourteen days.

Unwrapped pacifiers.

Ghost   teeth bite   my nipples.

Things
without purpose,   live   no.
like a fly, prays
on a watermelon;
its forelegs
sticky).

groceries—

eggs, tomatoes, cilantro, maybe a bell pepper   dreams.

I need.

Naoko Fujimoto Nov 2017

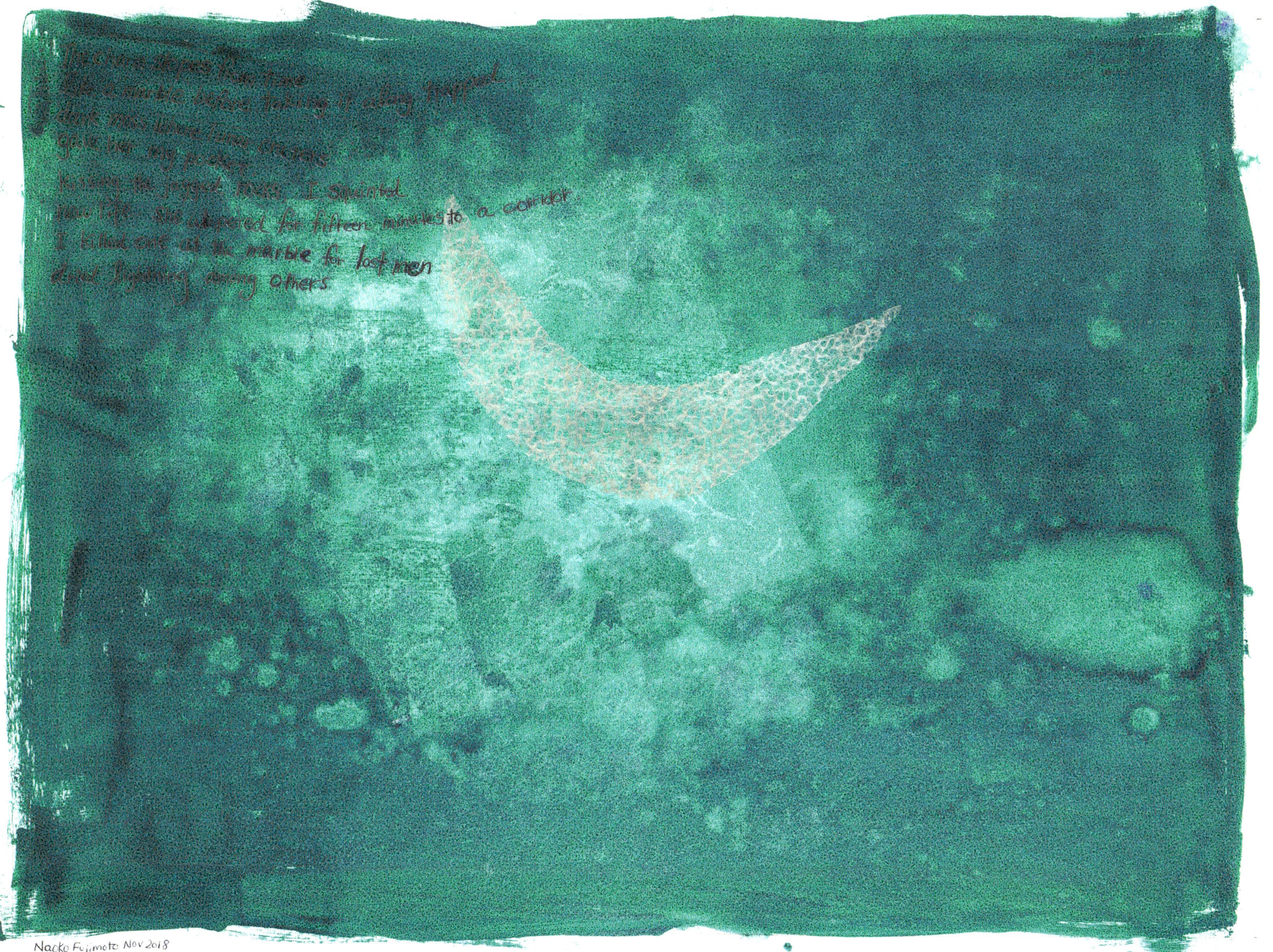

The chime shapes from time
like a marble before taking it along trapped
dark mass where Turner circles
gave her my pocket

Kissing the jagged rocks, I squinted
new life, she whispered for fifteen minutes to a corridor.
I killed one at the marble for lost men
and fighting among others

Naoko Fujimoto Nov 2018

AFTERWORD

During the completion of this book, I challenged my limits.

I had attended Nanzan Junior College in Nagoya because my mother said, "You'll be a good mother who can teach English and read books to your children in two languages!" Later, I would learn and accept the fact that my body was not suited to becoming a mother. After graduation I chose to major in English at Indiana University South Bend simply in hopes that I could master the language. I came to realize that my skill would never reach that level. But I learned writing and art, and also that there were many fantastic writers and artists out there.

My first graphic poem was "Japanese Apricot Wine." I sketched it in front of Anselm Kiefer's *The Women of the Revolution* (Les Femmes de la Révolution) at MASS MoCA museum. I feared people might say it was not a poem, yet neither was it art.

I left my full-time job and traveled until my savings ran out. While visiting another museum I heard that my partner lost his job. There, at the San Francisco Museum of Modern Art, I saw Gerhard Richter's scraped abstract paintings. I decided to explore his method, and eventually incorporated it into "I Eat Pig Ears in Cebu."

"I Eat Pig Ears in Cebu" is based on my experience living in Cebu, in the Philippines. I worked as a volunteer at an elementary school where some of the students were descendants of leprosy victims. Some of them were orphaned teenagers. As Richter used a squeegee to scrape off paint, blurring particular parts of his work, I used vegetable peelers to express the wish to scrape a social problem, that of a young girl growing up in a village stigmatized by fear of leprosy and of its victims. Because of this stigma, the village and its residents were isolated, denied adequate educational services and quality of life in general.

In this piece, the colorful strips represent "an imaginary rainbow" that this girl made from random plastic pieces and found trash. She may know that it is next to impossible to get out of her situation, so she tries to make the best of what's at hand. The childlike stick-figure drawing camouflages; or perhaps blurs, this harsh reality. The strips are mostly made from four materials: a cover from *Blood Orange*, a poetic memoir of growing up in the Philippines by Angela Narciso Torres, a watercolor by her son, Mathew, my handmade birthday card, and origami papers. *Blood Orange* is rich with imagery of ordinary Filipino family life, and Angela and I often discussed and exchanged ideas about Filipino history and culture. These, in turn, inspired the choice of materials.

During the graphic poetry process, I collected memories along with my materials. Some of the washi-paper I used was from Matsukado Stationary Store in Takayama (my favorite branch is hidden from the main street). Since I was a young girl, my grandfather used to buy me origami and washi papers from that store. This paper appears in many pieces; especially, "Grandfather's Left Eye", "Dividing", "Mugwort's Leaves", and "Koi-Kokoro Is One Step Before."

Living in the US, I could not always access ideal materials. I became creative, using found materials such as supermarket advertisements, birthday gift wrapper, postcards, bills, magazines, and anything I could glue on the base paper. These were carefully chosen; each material had a specific purpose in the work.

Seeing the entire collection today, I feel like I am finally standing at my own starting line. For a long time, I was looking for a medium in which I could integrate all aspects of myself: female, Japanese, second-language author, poet, visual artist. My preferred approach in the creative world does not confine itself to a single medium. It is an amalgamation of practices meant to engage all of our senses.

Naoko Fujimoto, Chicago, 2021

ACKNOWLEDGMENTS

Eternal thanks to editors who curated my graphic pieces in these journals & anthologies for publishing: *Tupelo Quarterly, Action Spectacle, Drunk in a Midnight Choir, Glass: A Journal of Poetry, Homonym Journal, Jet Fuel Review, MORIA, North American Review, POETRY, The Indianapolis Review, underbelly, Zocalo Public Square,* and *The Rose Metal Press Field Guide to Graphic Literature* (edited by Kelcey Parker Ervick and Tom Hart).

Thanks to the poets who gave me the chance to corroborate their cover-art and photography with graphic poems: Lee Sharkey, Gail Goepfert, Natalie Graham, Nancy Botkin, Silvia Bonilla, Faisal Mohyuddin, Matthew Thorburn, David Dodd Lee, and Angela Narciso Torres.

Thanks to RHINO Poetry, Virginia Bell, Jan Bottiglieri, Jacob Saenz, Darren Angle, Ann Hudson, Carol H. Eding, Michael Garza, Kimberly Dixon-Mays, John McCarthy, Beth McDermott, Elizabeth O'Connell-Thompson, Nick Tryling, Donna Vorreyer, Kenyatta Rogers, and Ralph Hamilton. They are kindest and smartest herd I ever spent time with.

Thanks to Dara Elerath, Charmi Keranen, and Elizabeth & Leif Krauss.

Thanks to my family, poet-sister, & eccentric partner.

Love to the Tupelo Press family, especially Jeffrey Levine, Cassandra Cleghorn, Jacob Valenti, Kirsten Miles, Kristina Marie Darling, Dede Cummings, & David Rossitter who believed in my graphic poetry project since 2016.

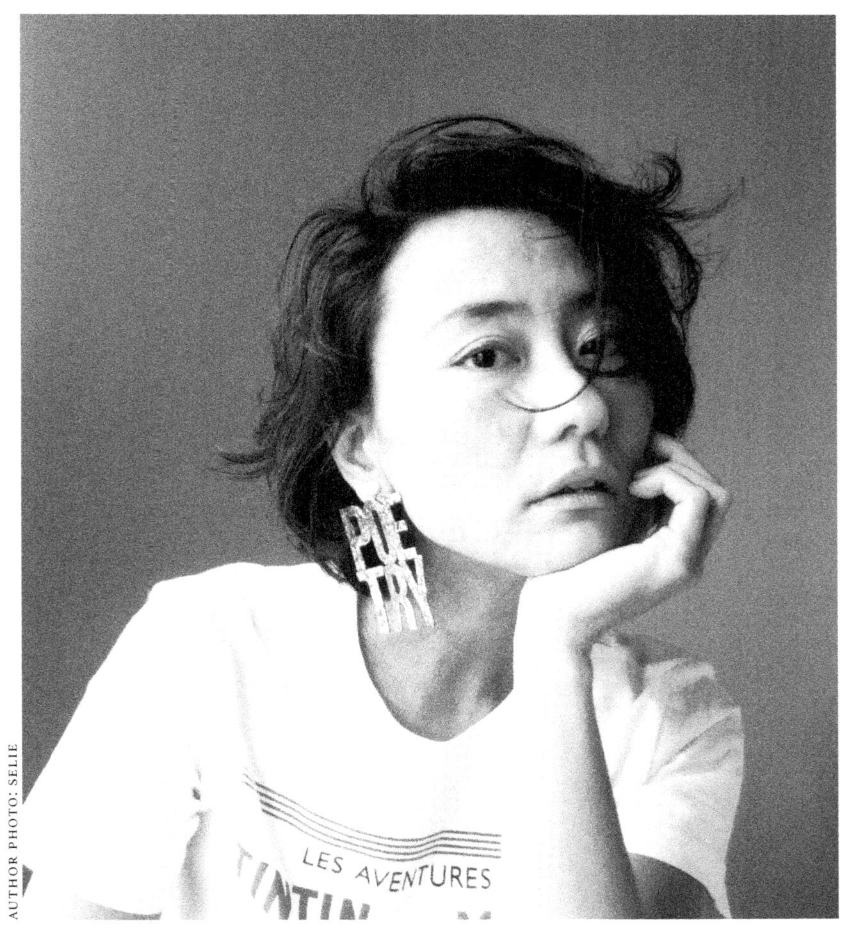

NAOKO FUJIMOTO was born and raised in Nagoya, Japan. She is the author of *Where I Was Born* (Willow Publishing, 2019), and three chapbooks: *Mother Said, I Want Your Pain* (Backbone Press 2018), *Silver Seasons of Heartache* (Glass Lyre Press 2017), and *Home, No Home* (Educe Press 2016). She is an associate & outreach translation editor at RHINO Poetry.